NUMBER 274

THE ENGLISH
EXPERIENCE

ITS RECORD IN EARLY PRINTED BOOKS
PUBLISHED IN FACSIMILE

GERRIT de VEER

THE TRUE AND PERFECT DESCRIPTION OF THREE VOYAGES BY THE SHIPS OF HOLLAND AND ZELAND

LONDON 1609

DA CAPO PRESS
THEATRVM ORBIS TERRARVM LTD.
AMSTERDAM 1970 NEW YORK

The publishers acknowledge their gratitude
to the Governors of the John Rylands Library
Manchester, M3 3EH
for their permission to reproduce
the Library's copy
(Shelfmark: 9869)

G
690
1594
'V4152

S.T.C.No. 24628
Collation: A^2, B-X^4

Published in 1970 by
Theatrum Orbis Terrarum Ltd.,
O.Z. Voorburgwal 85, Amsterdam
&
Da Capo Press
- a division of Plenum Publishing Corporation -
227 West 17th Street, New York, 10011
Printed in the Netherlands
ISBN 90 221 0274 2

THE
True and perfect De-
ſcription of three Voy-

ages, ſo ſtrange and woonderfull,
that the like hath neuer been
heard of before :
Done and performed three yeares, one after the other, by the Ships of
Holland and *Zeland*, on the North ſides of *Norway*, *Muſcouia* and
Tartaria, towards the Kingdomes of *Cathaia* & *China*; ſhewing
the diſcouerie of the Straights of *Weigates*, *Noua Zembla*,
and the Countrie lying vnder 80. degrees; which is
thought to be *Greenland* : where neuer any man had
bin before : with the cruell Beares, and other
Monſters of the Sea, and the vnſup-
portable and extreame cold
that is found to be in
thoſe places.
And how that in the laſt Voyage, the Shippe was ſo incloſed by the
Ice, that it was left there, whereby the men were forced to build a
houſe in the cold and deſart Countrie of *Noua Zembla*, wherin
they continued 10. monthes togeather, and neuer ſaw nor
heard of any man, in moſt great cold and extreame
miſerie; and how after that, to ſaue their liues, they
were conſtrained to ſayle aboue 350. Duch-
miles, which is aboue 1000. miles Engliſh,
in litle open Boates, along and ouer the
maine Seas, in moſt great daunger,
and with extreame labour, vn-
ſpeakable troubles, and
great hunger.

Imprinted at London for *T. Pauier*,
1609.

TO THE RIGHT WOR-
fhipfull, Sir *Thomas Smith* Knight, Gouernour of the *Muscouy* Company, &c.

RIGHT WORSHIPFVLL:

*Eing intreated by some of my Friends, and
principally by* M. Richard Hakluyt *(a diligent obseruer of all Proceedings in this nature) to Translate and publish these three
yeares Trauelles and Discoueries, of the* Hollanders *to the* North-easts *I could not deuise how to consecrate my Labours so properly
to any, as to your selfe, considering not onely*
*the generall good affection the whole Kingdome takes notice, that
you beare to all Honorable actions of this kinde, be they for Disco-
werie, Traffique, or Plantation; but also in respect of that particu-
lar charge, most worthily recommended to your care, ouer the Trade
of the* English *in those* North-east *Partes.*

*Many attempts and proffers (I confesse) there haue bin to find a
passage by those poorest parts, to the richest; by those barbarous, to
the most ciuile, those vnpeopled, to the most popular; those Desarts,
to the most fertile Conntries of the World: and of them all, none (I
dare say) vndertaken with greater iudgement, with more obdurate
Patience, euen* aduersus Elementa, aduersus ipsam in illis locis
rerum naturam, *then these three by the* Hollanders.

If any of our Nation *be employed that way in time to come, here
they haue a great part of their Voiage layd open, and the example of*

A ij.   *that*

The Epiſtle Dedicatorie.

that induſtrious people (firſt excited to this and other famous Voyages, by imitation of ſome of ours) for the conquering of all difficulties and dangers; thoſe people (I ſay) that of all Chriſtians, and for ought I know, of all Adams Poſteritie, haue firſt nauigated to 81. Degrees of Northerly Latitude, and wintered in 76. where they had no Inhabitants, but Foxes, Beares, and Deare, to keepe them company.

And were it for nothing elſe, but to regiſter the miraculous prouidence of the Creator, and his admirable and vnſpeakeable workes in theſe congealed Climats, vnknowen vtterly to the Ancients, and to demoſtrate how much we are obliged to his omnipotent fauour, for planting vs in ſo temperate, ſo ciuill, and ſo Religious a part of the World, as this bleſſed Iſland; I thinke omiſſion in this kinde were little leſſe then Sacriledge.

As it is, I humbly deſire you to vouch-ſafe it your protection, and to eſteeme mee,

Alwayes deuoted to your ſeruice,

WILLIAM PHILLIP.

The

The fyrst part of the Naui-
gation into the North Seas.

It is a most certaine and an assured assertion, that nothing doth more benefit and further the Common-wealth (specially these Countries) then the art and knowledge of Nauigation, in regard that such Countries and Nations as are strong and mightie at Sea, haue the meanes and ready way to draw, fetch, and bring vnto them for their maintenaunce, all the principalest commodities and fruites of the earth, for that thereby they are inabled to bring all necessary things for the nourishment and sustentation of man from the vttermost partes of the world, and to carry and conuay such wares and Marchandizes, (whereof they haue great store and aboundance) vnto the same places, which by reason of the art of Nauigation, and the commodities of the Sea, is easily to be effected and brought to passe. Which Nauigation as it dayly more & more increaseth (to the great woonder and admiration of those, that compare the Sea-faring & Nauigation vsed in our forefathers times, yea & that also that hath beene practised in our age, with that which now at this present is dayly furthered & sought out) so there are continually new voiages made, & strange Coasts discouered; the which although they be not done by the first, second, or third voiage, but after, by tract of time, first brought to their full effect, and desired commoditie, and the fruits thereof, by continuance of time reaped. Yet we must not be abasht, nor dismayed, at the labour, toile, trauaile, and dangers sustayned in such voiages, to that end made, although as I said before the benefit thereof be not had nor seene in the first, second, third, or more voiages, for what labour is more profitable, & worthier praise and commendation, then that which tendeth vnto the common good and benefit of all men? Although such as are vnskilfull, contemners, & deriders of mens diligence and proceedings therein, at the first esteeme it

As the art Nauigatio[n] more incre seth; so the are daily m new countr found out.

Diligence continuan effect tha which is sought.

We must leaue of t some men dislike or d praise in o proceeding

B.

an vnpꝛofitable and needleſſe thing, when as the end pꝛoouety veneſi-
ciall & commodious. If the famous Nauigatoꝛs Corteſius Nonius;
and Megalanes, & others, that in their times, ſought out and diſcouered the Kingdomes, Countries, and Ilands farre diſtant from vs, in
the extreameſt parts of the woꝛld; foꝛ the firſt, ſecond, oꝛ third voyage,
that had ſucceeded vnfoꝛtunately with them:had left off and giuen ouer
their nauigatiõ;they had not afterward reaped noꝛ enioyed the fruites,
beneſites,and commodities thereof. Alexander magnus (after he had
woone all Grecia,and from thence entred into little & great Aſia ; and
comming to the fartheſt parts of India, there found ſome difficultie
to paſſe) ſayd, If we had not gone foꝛward,and perſiſted in our intent,
which other men eſteemed and held to be impoſſible, we had ſtill re-
mayned and ſtayed in the entry of Cicilia,where as now we haue ouer-
runne & paſt thꝛough all thoſe large and ſpacious Countries : foꝛ nothing is found and effected all at one time, neither is any thing that is
put in pꝛactiſe, pꝛeſently bꝛought to an end. To the which end,Cicero
wiſely ſaith; God hath giuen vs ſome things,& not all things,that our
ſucceſſours alſo might haue ſomewhat to doe.Therefoꝛe we muſt not
leaue off,noꝛ ſtay our pꝛetence in the middle of our pꝛoceedinges, as
long as there is any commoditie to be hoped, & in time to be obtayned:
foꝛ that the greateſt and richeſt treaſures are hardlieſt to be found.But
to make no long digreſſion from our matter,concerning the dayly fur-
theraunce of the moſt neceſſarie and pꝛofitable art of Nauigation,that
hath been bꝛought to full effect, not without great charges, labour,
and paines; ouerſlipping and not ſhewing with how long and trouble-
ſome labour and toyle, continually had, the paſſages to the Eaſt and
Weſt Indies, America,Braſilia, and other places, thꝛough the ſtraight
of Magellanes, in the South ſea, twiſe oꝛ thꝛiſe paſſing vnder the
Line,and by thoſe meanes other Countries & Ilands,were firſt found
out and diſcouered.

Let vs looke into the White Seas, that are now ſo commonly
ſayled (on the noꝛth ſide of Muſconia) with what cumberſome labour
and toyle,they were firſt diſcouered : What hath now made this Uoyage ſo common and eaſie ? is it not the ſame, and as long a voyage as
it was, befoꝛe it was fully knowne and found out ? J, but the right
courſes, which at the firſt were to be ſought, by croſſing the Seas
from one Land to another, & are now to be held aloofe into the Seas,
and directly ſayled ; hath of difficult and toyleſome, made them eaſie
                                                                    and

thing not
ntinued,
ꝛ not be
ꞓcted.

l things are
ꞓcted in
nuenient
me.

hat which in
e beginning
hard, by
ontinuance
f time is
ꝛade eaſie
ad light.

and ready Uoyages.

This small Discourse I thought good to set downe, for an intro-
duction vnto the Reader, in regard that I haue vndertaken to describe
the Three Uoyages made into the North Seas, in three yeares, one
after the other; behind Norway, and along and about Muscouia, towardes the Kingdome of Cathaia and China : whereof, the two last,
I my selfe holpe to effect; and yet brought them not to the desired
end that we well hoped.

First, to shew our diligent, and most toylesome labour and paynes
taken, to find out the right course; which we could not bring to passe,
as we well hoped, wished, and desired, and possible might haue found
it, by crossing the Seas, if we had taken the right course; if the Ice
and the shortnesse of time, and bad crosses had not hindered vs : And
also to stoppe their mouthes, that report and say, that our proceeding
therein, was wholly vnprofitable and fruiteless; which peraduenture
in time to come, may turne vnto our great profite and commoditie. For
he which proceedeth and continueth in a thing that seemeth to be impossible, is not to be discommended : but hee, that in regarde that the
thing seemeth to be impossible, doth not proceed therein, but by his
faint heartednesse and sloath, wholly leaueth it off.

The first fin-
ding is hard,
but the secon
attempt is
easier.

Wee haue assuredly found, that the onely and most hinderaunce to
our voyage, was the Ice, that we found about Noua Zembla, vnder
73.74.75. and 76. degrees; and not so much vpon the Sea betweene
both the Landes : whereby it appeareth, that not the nearenesse of the
North pole, but the Ice that commeth in and out from the Tartarian
Sea, about Noua Zembla, caused vs to feele the greatest cold. Therefore in regard that the nearenesse of the Pole was not the cause of the
great cold that we felt, if we had had the meanes to haue held our ap-
poynted and intended course into the North-east, we had peraduenture found some enteraunce : which course we could not hold from
Noua Zembla, because that there we entred amongst great store of
Ice ; and how it was about Noua Zembla, we could not tell, before
we had sought it; and when we had sought it, we could not then alter
our course, although also it is vncertaine, what we should haue done, if
we had continued in our North-east course, because it is not yet found
out. But it is true, that in the Countrie lying vnder 80. degrees,
(which we esteeme to be Greenland) there is both Leaues and Grasse
to be seene : Wherein, such Beastes as feed of Leaues and Grasse, (as

Not the
nearenes of
the North
pole, but the
Ice in the
Tartarian sea
causeth the
greatest cold

Partes,

parts, Hindes, and such like beastes liue, whereas to the contrary In noua Zembla, there groweth nether leaues nor grasse, and there are no beasts therein but such as eate flesh, as Beares, & Foxes, &c. Although Noua Zembla, lyeth 4.5. and 6. degrees more Southerly from the

A comparison of the heate vnder the line, with the cold vnder the North Pole.

pole, then the other land aforesaid. It is also manifest, that vpon the South and North side of the line of the sunne on both sides, between both the Tropicos, vnder 23. degrees and a halfe, it is as hot, as it is right vnder the Line. What wonder then should it be, that about the North Pole also, and as many degrees on both sides, it should not bee colder then right vnder the Pole: I will not affirme this to bee true, because that the colde on both sides of the North Pole hath not as yet beene discouered and sought out, as the heat on the North and South side of the line hath beene. Onely thus much I will say, that although we held not our direct pretended course to the North-east, that therefore it is to be iudged, that the cold would haue let our passage through that way, for it was not the Sea, nor the neerenesse vnto the Pole, but the Ice about the land, that let & hindered vs (as I sayd before) for that as soone as we made from the land, & put more into the sea, although it

The resolute intent and opinions of William Barents.

was much further Northward, presently we felt more warmth, and in ý opinion our Pilote William Barents dyed, who notwithstanding the feareful and intollerable cold that he indured, yet he was not discouraged, but offered to lay wagers with diuers of vs, that by Gods helpe, he would bring that pretended voiage to an end, if he held his course North-east from the North Cape. But I will leaue that, and shewe you, of the three Voyages aforesaid, begun and set forth by the permission and furtherance of the generall States of the vnited Prouinces, and of Prince Maurice, as Admirall of the Sea, and the rich Towne of Amsterdam. Whereby the Reader may iudge and conceaue what is to bee done, for the most profite and aduantage, and what is to be left.

First you must vnderstand, that in Anno 1594. there was 4. ships set foorth out of the vnited Prouinces, whereof two were of Amsterdam; one of Zelandt, and one of Enckhuysen, that were appointed to saile into the North Seas, to discouer the Kingdomes of Cathaia, and China; North-ward from Norway, Muscouia, and about Tartaria, whereof William Barents, a notable skilfull and wise Pilote, was Commander ouer the Ships of Amsterdam, and with them vpon Whit-sunday departed from Amsterdam and went to the Texel.

Vpon

Upon the fifth of June they failed out of the Texel, and hauing a good wind and faire weather, vpon the 23. of June, they arriued at Kilduin in Muscouia, which for that it is a place well knowen and a common Voyage, I will make no further discription thereof.

The 29. of June, at foure of the clocke in the after noone, they set faile out of Kilduin, and so 13. or 14. miles out-right, failed North-eaft, with a north north-weft wind, and close weather.

The 30. of June they sayled Eaft North-eaft 7. miles, till the Sunne was Eaft South-eaft, with an North wind, with 2. Schower failes, there they caft out their lead, at 100. fadome deepth, but found no ground.

From whence the same day they failed Eaft north-eaft 5. miles, till the Sunne was full South, hauing the wind North with 2. Schower failes, where once againe they caft out the lead 100. fadome deepe, but found no ground, and then from noone to night the same day, they sai-led Eaft, & Eaft and by North 13. miles, till the Sunne was North-weft, and there cafting out their lead, they had ground at 120. fadome, the ground being oafie, and blacke durt.

The 1. of July, after they had failed one quarter 4. miles Eaft, and Eaft and by North, early in the morning they caft out the lead, & found ground at 60. fadome, where they had an oafie small sandy ground, and within an houre after they caft out the lead againe, and had ground at 52. fadome, being white sand mixed with blacke, and some-what oafie: after that they failed 3. miles Eaft and by North, where they had ground at 40. fadome, being gray sand mixed with white. From thence they failed 2. miles Eaft-ward, with a North north-eaft winde, there they had ground at 38. fadome, being red sand mixed with black, the Sunne being South-eaft and by eaft. From thence they failed 3. miles, Eaft and by South, & Eaft South-eaft til noone, where they had the Sunne at 70. degrees and ¼. there they caft out the lead a-gaine, and had ground at 39. fadome, being small gray sand, mixed with blacke ftippelen and peeces of Shels.

Then againe they failed 2. miles South-eaft, and then woond North-ward with an Eaft north-eaft wind, and after failed 6. miles North-eaft all that day, with a South-eaft wind, till the Sunne was North North-weft, the weather being cold, and the lead being caft foorth they found ground at 60. fadome, being small gray oafie sand, mixed with a little blacke, and great whole shels: after that the same Euening to the

firſt quarter, they ſailed 5. miles, Eaſt no?th-eaſt, and No?th-eaſt and
by Eaſt, and after that Eaſt no?th-eaſt, and No?th-eaſt and by Eaſt 5.
miles, vntill the ſecond of July in the Mo?ning, and there they had 65.
fadome deepe, the ground oaſie with blacke ſlime o? durt.

The ſame day from Mo?ning to Noone, they ſailed 3. o? 4. miles
Eaſt no?th-eaſt, the wind blowing ſtiffe South-eaſt, whereby at
Noone they were fo?ced to table in the fo?e-ſaile, and d?iue with a
Schower ſaile, in miſtie weather, fo? the ſpace of 3. o? 4. miles, vntill
Euening, holding Eaſt, and Eaſt and by South, after that the winde
blew South-weſt, and about 5. of the clocke in the after-noone, they
caſt out the lead, but had no ground at 120. fadome. That Euening
the weather cleared vp againe, and they ſailed about 5. miles befo?e
the wind Eaſt no?th-eaſt, fo? the ſpace of 3. houres, and then againe it
began to be miſtie, ſo that they durſt not ſaile fo?ward, but lay hulling
in the wind, where vpon Sunday mo?ning being the 3. of July, when
the Sunne was No?th-eaſt, they caſt out the lead and found ground
at 125. fadome, being blacke durt o? ſlime.

From thence they ſailed 8. Miles Eaſt No?th-eaſt, till the Sunne
was South-eaſt, and caſting out the lead, found ground at 140. fadom,
being blacke ſlimie durt, at which time they tooke the high of the Sun
and found it to be 73. degrees and 6. minutes, & p?eſently againe they
caſt out the lead, and had 130. fadome decpth, the ground being blacke
ſlime. After that they ſapled 6. o? 7. miles further Eaſt no?th-eaſt, till
the Sunne was No?th-weſt.

On Sunday in the Mo?ning being the 3. of July, it was very
faire and cleare weather, the wind blowing South-weſt, at which time
William Barents found out the right Meridien, taking the high of the
Sunne with his Croſſe-ſtaffe when it was South-eaſt, and found
it to be eleuated in the South-eaſt 28. degrees and a halfe, and when it
had paſt ouer Weſt & by No?th, it was but 28. degrees & a half aboue
the Ho?izon, ſo that it differed 5. points and a half, which being deuided
there reſted 2. points and ¼. ſo that their compaſſe was altered 2. points,
and ¼. as it appeared the ſame day, when the ſunne was in her higth betweene South ſouth-weſt, and ſouth-weſt and by ſouth, fo? the Sun
was ſouth-weſt and by ſouth, and yet was not declined, and they had
73. degrees and 6. minutes.

The 4. of July in the mo?ning, they ſailed 4. Miles eaſt and by
no?th, and caſting out the lead found ground at 125 fadome being ſlimie.

mle. That night the weather was miftie againe, and in the Mozning the winde was eaft, then they failed 4. miles South-eaft and by fouth, till the Sunne was eaft, and then againe they caft out the lead, & found ground at 108. fadome, blacke durt, then they wound nozth-ward, & failed 6. Miles, nozth nozth-eaft, and nozth-eaft and by nozth, untill the Sunne was fouth fouth-weft, and then they faw the Land of Noua Zembla, lying South-eaft and by Eaft 6. oz 7. miles from them, where they had blacke durty ground at 105. fadome. Then they wound fouth-ward againe, and failed 6. Miles, fouth and by Weft, till the Sunne was Weft nozth-weft, there they had 68. Fadome deepe, with durtie ground as befoze the wind being fouth-eaft.

Then they wound Eaft-ward & failed 6. Miles eaft and by fouth, at which time, William Barents tooke the heigth of the Sunne with his Croffe-ftaffe, wheu it was at the loweft, that is between nozth nozth-eaft, and eaft and by nozth, and found it to bee eleuated aboue the Hozizon 6. degrees & ⅓. part, his declination being 12. degrees & 55. minuts, from whence fubftracting the afozefaid heigth, there refteth 16. degrees and 35. minutes, which being fubftracted from 90. degrees, there refteth 73. degrees and 25. minutes which was, when they were about 5. oz 6. miles from the Land of Noua Zembla.

Then they wound eaft-ward and failed 5. miles, eaft & by fouth, and eaft South-eaft, and paft by a long point of Land that lay out into the fea, which they named Langenes, and hard by that point Eaft-ward, there was a great Bay, where they went a land with their boate, but found no people.

Thzee oz foure Miles from Langenes eaft nozth-eaft, there lay a long point, and a Mile eaft-ward from the faid point there was a great Bay, and vpon the eaft-fide of the faid Bay, there lay a Rock not very high aboue the water, and on the Weft-fide of the Bay, there ftood a fharpe little hill, eafie to be knowne, befoze the Bay, it was 20. fadome deepth, the ground fmall blacke ftones, like peafe : from Langenes to Cape Bapo Eaft nozth-eaft it is 4. miles.

From Cape Bapo to the Weft point of Lombsbay nozth-eaft and by nozth are 5. miles, and betweene them both there are 2. Creekes. Lombsbay is a great wide Bay, on the Weft-fide thereof hauing a faire Hauen 6. 7. oz 8. fadome deepe, blacke fand, there they went on fhoze with their boate, & vpon the fhoze placed a beacon, made of an old Maft which they found there; Calling the Bay Lombsbay, becaufe of
a cer-

a certaine kind of Beares so called, which they found there in great aboundance.

The East point of Lombsbay, is a long narrow point, & by it there lyeth an Island, and from that long point to Sea-ward in, there is a great Creeke. This Lombsbay lyeth vnder 74. Degrees and ⅓. part. From Lombsbay to the point of the Admirals Island, they sailed 6, or 7. Miles, North-east and by North. The Admirals Island is not very faire one the East-side, but a farre off very flat, so that you must shunne it long before you come at it, it is also very vneuen, for at one casting off the lead they had 10. fadome deepe, and presently at another casting of the lead they had but 6. fadome, and presently after that againe 10, 11. and 12. fadome, the streame running hard against the flats.

From the East-end of the Admirals Island, to Cape Negro, that is the Blacke point, they sailed about 5. or 6. Miles, East North-east, and a Mile without the Black point it is 70. fadome deepe, the ground flimie, as vpon Pamphius, right East-ward of the Blacke point, there are 2. sharpe pointed hilles in the Creeke, that are easie to be knowen. The 6. of July, the Sunne being North, they came right before the Blacke point with faire weather, this Blacke point lyeth vnder 75. Degrees and 20. minutes. From the Blacke point to Williams Island, they sailed 7. or 8. Miles, East North-east, and between them both about halfe a Mile, there lay a small Island.

The 7. of July they sailed from Williams Island, and then William Barents tooke the height of the Sunne, with his Crosse-staffe, and found it to be eleuated aboue the Horizon in the south-west and by south 53. Degrees and 6. minutes, his declination being 22. Degrees and 49. minutes, which being added to 53. Degrees and 6. minutes, make 75. Degrees and 55. minutes. This is the right height of the Pole of the said Island. In this Island they found great store of Driff-wood, & many Sea-horses being a kinde of fish that keepeth in the Sea, hauing very great teeth, which at this day are vsed insteed of Iuorie or Elophants teeth, there also is a good road for ships, at 12. & 13. fadome deepe against all winds, except it be West south-west, and West windes, and there they found a piece of a Russia ship, and that day they had the wind East North-east, mistie weather.

The 9. of July they entered into Beeren-fort, vpon the road vnder Williams Island, and there they found a white Beare, which they per-

perceiuing, presently entered into their Boate, and shot her into the body with a musket, but the Beare shewed most wonderfull strength, which almost is not to be found in any beast, for no man euer heard the like to be done by any Lyon or cruel beast whatsoeuer: for notwithstanding that she was shot into the bodie, yet she leapt vp, & swame in the water, the men that were in the boate rowing after her, cast a rope about her necke, and by that meanes drew her at the sterne of the boat, for that not hauing seene the like Beare before, they thought to haue carryed her aliue in the shippe, and to haue shewed her for a strange wonder in Holland; but she vsed such force, that they were glad that they were rid of her, and contented themselues with her skin only, for she made such a noyse, and stroue in such sort, that it was admirable, wherewith they let her rest and gaue her more scope, with the rope that they held her by, and so drew her in that sort after them, by that meanes to wearie her: meane time, William Barents made neerer to her, but the Beare swome to the boate, and with her fore-feet got hold of the sterne thereof, which William Barents perceiuing, said, she will there rest her selfe, but she had another meaning, for she vsed such force, that at last she had gotten halfe her body into the boat, wherewith the men were so abashed, that they run into þ further end of the boate, and thought verily to haue been spoiled by her, but by a strange meanes they were deliuered from her, for that the rope that was about her necke, caught hold vpon the hooke of the Ruther, whereby the Beare could get no further, but so was held backe, and hanging in that manner, one of the men boldly stept foorth from the end of the Scute, and thrust her into the bodie with a Halfe-pike; & therewith she fell downe into the water, and so they rowed forward with her to the ship, drawing her after them, till shee was in a manner dead, wherewith they killed her out-right, and hauing fleaed her, brought the skinne to Amsterdam.

The 20. of July, they sailed out of Beren-fort frō Williams Iland, & the same day in the morning got to the Iland of Crosses, and there went on land with their Pinnace, and found the Iland to bee barren, and full of Cliffes and Rocks, in it there was a small Hauen, whereinto they rowed with their boat. This Iland is about halfe a Mile long, and reacheth East and West; on the West end it hath a Banke, about a third part of a Mile long, and at the East end also another Banke, vpon this Iland there standeth 2. great Crosses, the Iland

lyeth

lyeth about 2.long Miles from the firme land,and vnder the Eaſt-end thereof there is good road,at 26. fadome ſoft ground; and ſomewhat cloſer to the Iſland on the Strand, at 9.fadome ſandy ground.

From the Iſland of Croſſes to the point of Cape Naſſawe, they ſailed eaſt,and eaſt and by north about 8.miles: it is a long flat point which you muſt bee carefull to ſhunne, for thereabouts at 7. fadome there were flats or ſholes, very farre from the Land; It lyeth almoſt vnder 76. Degrees and a halfe. From the Weſt-end of Williams Iſland,to the Iſland with the Croſſes is 3. miles, the courſe North.

From Naſſaw point they ſailed Eaſt and by South, and eaſt ſouth-eaſt 5.miles,& then they thought that they ſaw land in North-eaſt and by Eaſt,& ſailed towards it 5.miles North-eaſt to deſcrie it,thinking it to be another land, that lay north-ward from Noua Zembla, but it began to blow ſo hard out of the Weſt, that they were forced to take in their Marſaile, & yet the wind roſe in ſuch manner, that they were forced to take in all their ſailes, and the ſea went ſo hollow,that they were conſtrained to driue 16.houres together without ſaile 8. or 9.Miles Eaſt north-eaſt.

The 11. of July their boat was by a great waue of the ſea ſunke to the ground, and by that meanes they loſt it, and after that they draue without ſailes 5.miles, Eaſt and by South; at laſt the Sunne being almoſt South-eaſt, the wind came about to the North-weſt, and then the weather began ſomewhat to cleare vp, but yet it was very miſtie. Then they hoyſed vp their ſailes againe and ſailed 4. Miles till night, that the Sunne was North and by Eaſt, and there they had 60. fadome deepth, muddie ground, and then they ſaw certaine flakes of Ice, at which time vpon the 12. of July they woond weſt, and held North-weſt, and ſailed about a mile with miſtie weather, and a north-weſt wind,and ſailed vp & downe weſt ſouth-weſt 3.or 4.Miles to ſee if they could find their boat againe : after that they wound againe with the wind,and ſayled 4.miles ſouth-eaſt,till the ſunne was ſouth-weſt, and then they were cloſe by the Land of Noua Zembla, that lay Eaſt and by North, and Weſt & by ſouth; from thence they wound ouer againe till noone and ſayled 3. Miles, North and by Weſt, and then till the Sunne was North-weſt, they held North-weſt and by North 3.Miles,then they waund Eaſt-ward and ſailed 4.or 5. Miles north-eaſt,and by eaſt.

The 13. of July at night, they found great ſtore of Ice,as much as
the

they could descrie out of the top, that lay as if it had been a plaine field of Ice, then they wound West-ward ouer from the Ice, and sailed about 4. miles West south-west, till the Sunne was east and by north, and that they saw the Land of Noua Zembla, lying South south-east from them.

Then they wound North-ward againe and sailed 2. Miles, till the Sunne was East south-east, and then againe found great store of Ice, and after that sailed South-west and by south 3. miles.

The 14. of July, they wound North-ward againe, & sayled with 2. Schower sailes North and by East, and North north-east 5. or 6. Miles, to the height of 77. Degrees and ⅓ part, and entred againe amongst the Ice, being so broad that they could not see ouer it, there they had no ground at 100. fadome, and then it blew hard West north-west.

From thence they wound South-ward, and sailed South south-west 7. or 8. miles, & came againe by the land that shewed to be 4. or 5. high hilles. Then they wound Northward, and till Euening sayled North 6. Miles, but there againe they found Ice.

From thence they wound South-ward and sailed South and by west 6. miles, and then againe entred into Ice.

The 15. of July, they wound South-ward againe, sayling South and by west 6. miles, and in the Morning, were by the land of Noua Zembla againe, the Sunne being about North-east.

From thence they wound North-ward againe, and sayled North and by east 7. miles, and entred againe into the Ice. Then they wound South-ward againe, the Sunne being west and sailed South south-west, and south-west and by south 8. or 9. miles, vpon the 16. of July.

From thence they wound North-ward, and sailed north and by east 4. miles, after that againe they wound west-ward and sailed West and by south 4. miles, and then they sailed north north-west 4. miles, and then the wind blew north north-east, and it froze hard; this was vpon the 17. of July.

Then they wound East-ward, and sailed East till noone, 3. Miles, and after that east and by south 3. Miles; from thence about Euening they wound northward & sailed north and by east 5. miles, till the 18. of July in the morning then they sailed north & by west 4. miles, & there entred againe amongst a great many flakes of Ice, from whence they wound southward, & close by the Ice they had no ground at 150. fadom.

C 2   Then

Then they ſayled about 2. houres South-eaſt, and Eaſt ſouth-eaſt, with myſtie weather, & came to a ſtake of Ice, which was ſo broad that they could not ſee ouer it, it being faire ſtill weather, and yet it froze, and ſo ſailed along by the Ice 2. houres; after that it was ſo miſtie, that they could ſee nothing round about them, and ſailed South-weſt two Miles.

The ſame day William Barents tooke the height of the Sun, with his Aſtrolabium, and then they were vnder 77. degrees and a ¼ of the Pole, and ſailed South-ward 6. Miles, and perceiued the firme land, lying South from them.

Then they ſailed till the 19. of July in the Morning, Weſt ſouth-weſt, 6. or 7. miles, with a North-weſt wind, and miſtie weather, & after that South-weſt and ſouth-weſt and by weſt 7. miles, the Sunne being 77. degrees 5. minutes leſſe. Then they ſailed 2. miles South-weſt, & were cloſe by the land of Noua Zembla, about Cape Naſſauc.

From thence they wound north-ward, & ſailed north 8. miles, with a Weſt north-weſt wind, and a miſt, and till the 20. of July in the Morning North-eaſt and by north 3. or 4. miles, and when the Sunne was eaſt they wound Weſt, and till Euening ſailed South-weſt 5. or 6. miles, with miſtie weather, and then ſouth-weſt and by ſouth 7. miles, till the 21. of July in the Morning.

Then they wound North-ward againe, and from Morning till euening ſailed North-weſt and by weſt 9. Miles, with miſtie weather, and againe north-weſt and by weſt 3. miles, and then wound South-ward, and till the 22. of July in the Morning ſailed South South-weſt 3. Miles, with miſtie weather, and till euening South and by Weſt, 9. Miles, all miſtie weather.

After that they wound North-ward againe, and ſailed North-weſt and by North 3. Miles, and then 2. Miles north-weſt, and in the morning being the 23. of July the wind blew North-weſt, and then they caſt out the lead, and had 48. fadome muddie ground.

Then they ſailed 2. Miles North north-eaſt and North & by Eaſt, and 2. Miles North-eaſt, at 46. fadome deepe, after that they wound Weſt-ward, and ſailed weſt and by north 6. miles, there it was 60. fadome deepe, muddy ground.

Then they wound Eaſtward and ſailed 3. miles Eaſt and by north, then againe 9. or 10. miles eaſt and eaſt & by South, and after that 5. or 6. miles Eaſt and eaſt and by ſouth, & after that 5. or 6. miles more, eaſt and

and by ſouth, till euening, being the 24. of July, then againe 4. Miles South-eaſt and by eaſt, the wind being eaſt North-eaſt.

Then they woond North-ward, and till the 25. of July in the Morning ſailed North and north and by Weſt 4. miles, there they had 130. fadome deepe muddie ground; then they ſailed north-ward where they had 100. fadome deepe, and there they ſaw the Ice in the North-eaſt, and then againe they ſailed 2. miles, North and by Weſt.

Then they woond South-ward, towards the Ice, and ſailed ſouth-eaſt one mile; after that they wound North-ward againe, and ſailed North 6. Miles, and were ſo incloſed about with flakes of Ice, that out of the top they could not diſcerne any thing beyond it, and ſought to get through the Ice, but they could not paſſe beyond it, and therefore in the euening they wound ſouth-ward againe, and ſailed along by the Ice, ſouth & by weſt 5. miles, & after that ſouth ſouth-eaſt 3. miles.

The 25. of July at night, they tooke the heigth of the Sunne, when it was at the loweſt between North and north-eaſt, and north-eaſt and by north, it being eleuated aboue the Horizon 6. degrees, and ⅓ his declinatiõ being 19. degrees 50. minutes, now take 6. degrees ⅓ from. 19. degrees and 50. minuts, and there reſteth 13. degrees 5. minutes, which ſubſtracted from 90. there reſteth 77. degrees leſſe 5. minutes.

The 26. of July, in the Morning they ſailed 6. miles South ſouth-eaſt, till the Sunne was South-weſt, & then South-eaſt 6. miles, and were within a mile of the land of Noua Zembla, & then wound north-ward from the land and ſailed 5. miles North-weſt with an eaſt wind, but in the Euening they wound South-ward againe, and ſailed ſouth-ſouth-eaſt 7. Miles, and were cloſe by the Land.

Then they wound north-ward againe, and ſailed North north-eaſt 2. or 3. Miles: from thence they wound South-ward, and ſailed South ſouth-eaſt 2. or 3. Miles, and came againe to Cape Truſt.

Then they wound againe from the Land, North-eaſt, about halfe a mile, and were ouer againſt the ſandes of 4. fadome deepe, betweene the rocke and the land, and there the ſands were 10. fadome deepe, the ground being ſmall blacke ſtones; then they ſailed North-weſt a little while, till they had 43. fadome deepe ſoft ground.

From thence they ſailed North-eaſt 4. Miles, vpon the 27. of July, with an Eaſt ſouth-eaſt wind, and wound South-ward againe, Where they found 70. fadome deepe, clay ground, and ſayled ſouth, and South and by Eaſt 4. miles, and came to a great Creek; & a Mile

C 3

and

and a halfe, from thence there lay a banke of sand of 18. fadome deepe, clay sandy ground, and betweene that sand or banke & the land, it was 60. and 50. fadome deepe, the coast reaching east and west by the Compasse.

In the euening they wound stife North-ward, and sailed 3. Miles North north-east; that day it was mistie, and in the night cleare, and William Barents tooke the height of the sunne with his Crosse-staffe, and found it to be eleuated aboue the Horizon 5. degrees 40. minutes, his declination being 19. degrees 25. minutes, from whence substracting 5. Degrees 40. minutes, there resteth 13. Degrees 45. minutes, which substracted from 90. rested 76. Degrees 31. minutes, for the height of the Pole.

Upon the 28. of July, they sailed 3. miles North north-east, and after that wound South-ward, and sailed 6. miles South south-east, and yet were then 3. or 4. miles from the land.

The 28. of July, the height of the sun being taken at noone, with the Astrolabiu, it was found to be eleuated aboue the Horizon 57 degrees & 6. minutes, her declination being 19. degrees & 18 minutes, which in all is 76. degrees and 24. minutes, they being then about 4. miles from the land of Noua Zembla, that lay all couered ouer with Snow, the weather being cleare, and the wind East.

Then againe (the Sunne being about South-west) they wound North-ward and sailed one mile North North-east, and then wound againe, and sailed another mile South-east, then they wound Northward againe, and sailed 4. miles North-east and North-east and by North.

The same day the height of the sunne being taken it was found to be 76. Degrees and 24. minutes, & then they sailed North-east 3. Miles, & after that North-east and by east 4. miles, and vpon the 29. of July came into the Ice againe.

The 29. of July the height of the Sunne being taken with the Crosse-Staffe, Astrolabium, and Quadrant, they found it to bee eleuated aboue the Horizon 32. degrees, her declination being 19. Degrees, which substracted from 32. there resteth 13. Degrees of the Equator, which being substracted from 90. there rested 77. Degrees, and then the neerest north point of Noua Zembla, called the ice point, lay right East from them.

There

There they found certaine Stones that glittered like gold, which for that cause they named gold-Stones, and there also they had a faire Bay with sandy ground.

Upon the same day they wound South-ward againe, and sailed South-east 2. miles betweene the Land and the Ice, and after that from the Ice point East, and to the South-ward 6. Miles to the Islands of Orange; and there they laboured forward betweene the Land and the Ice, with faire still weather, and vpon the 31. of July got to the Islands of Orange. And there went to one of those Islands, where they found about 200. Walrushen or Sea-horses, lying vpon the shoare to baste themselues in the sunne. This Sea-horse is a wonderfull strong monster of the sea, much bigger then an Oxe, which keepes continually in the seas, hauing a skinne like a Sea-calfe or Seale, with very short haire, mouthed like a Lyon, and many times they lie vpon the Ice; they are hardly killed vnlesse you strike them iust vpon the fore-head, it hath foure feet, but no eares, and commonly it hath one or two yong ones at a time. And when the Fisher-men chance to finde them vpon a flake of Ice with their yong ones, shee casteth her yong ones before her into the water, and then takes them in her armes and so plungeth vp and downe with them, and when shee will reuenge her selfe vpon the boats, or make resistance against them, then she casts her yong ones from her againe, & with all her force goeth towards the Boate, (whereby our men were once in no small danger, for that the Sea-horse had almost stricken her teeth into the sterne of their Boate) thinking to ouerthrowe it, but by meanes of the great cry that the men made, shee was afraid, and swomme away againe, and tooke her yong ones againe in her armes. They haue two teeth sticking out of their mouthes on each side one, each beeing about halfe an Elle long, and are esteemed to bee as good as any Iuorie or Elophants teeth, specially in Muscouia, Tartaria, and there abouts where they are knowne, for they are as white, hard, and euen as Iuory.

Those Sea-horses that lay bathing themselues vpon the Land, our men supposing that they could not defend themselues beeing out of the water, went on shoare to assaile them, and fought with thē, to get their teeth that are so rich, but they brake all their Hatchets, Curtle-axes, and Pikes in pieces, and could not kill one of them, but strucke some of their teeth out of their mouthes, which they tooke with them: and when they could get nothing against them by fighting, they

agreed

agreed to goe aboard the Ship, to fetch some of their great Ordinance, to shoot at them therewith, but it began to blow so hard, that it rent the Ice into great peices, so that they were forced not to do it, & therewith they found a great white Beare that slept, which they shot into the body, but she ranne away, and entred into the water; the men following her with their boat, and kil'd her out-right, and then drew her vpon the Ice, and so sticking a halfe pike vp-right, bound her fast vnto it, thinking to fetch her when they came backe againe, to shoot at the Seahorses with their Ordinance, but for that it began more and more to blow, and the Ice therewith brake in peeces, they did nothing at all.

After that W. Barents had begun this voyage vpon the fifth of Iune, 1594. and at that time (as I sayd before) set saile out of the Texell, the 23. of the same month arriuing at Kilduin in Muscouia, and from thence tooke his course on the North side of Noua Zembla, wherein he continued till the first of August, with such aduentures as are before declared, till he came to the Island of Orange: after he had taken all that paine, and finding that he could hardly get through, to accomplish and ende his pretended Voyage, his men also beginning to bee

There returne back againe. weary and would saile no further, they all together agreed to returne back againe, to meet with the other ships that had taken their course to the Weygates, or the Straights of Nassawe, to know what discoueries they had made there.

The first of August they turned their course to saile backe againe from the Islands of Orange, and sailed west and west by south 6. miles to the Ice point.

From the Ice point to the Cape of Comfort, they sailed West and somewhat South 30. Miles, betweene them both there lyeth very high Land, but the Cape of Comfort is very low flat land, and on the west end thereof there standeth foure or fiue blacke houels or little hilles like country houses.

Vpon the 3. of August, from the Cape of Comfort they wound North-ward, and sailed 8. Miles north-west, and by north, and North north-west, and about Noone they wound South-ward, till euening, and sailed south and by west, & south-south-west 7. Miles, & then came to a long narrow point of land one Cape Nassaw.

In the Euening they wound North-ward againe, and sailed north and by east 2. Miles, then the winde came North, and therefore they wound West-ward againe, & sailed North north-west one Mile, then the wind turned eaft, and with that they failed from the 4. of Auguft in the Mozning till Noone Weft and by nozth 5. oz 6. Miles, after that they failed till Euening South-weft 5. Miles, and after that South-weft 2. Miles moze, and fell vpon a low flat land which on the eaft-end had a white patche oz peece of ground.

After that they failed till Mozning, being the 5. of Auguft, Weft fouth-weft, 5. miles, then fouth-weft, 14. Miles, and then Weft 3. miles till the 6. of Auguft.

The 6. of Auguft they failed Weft fouth-weft, 2. oz 3. Miles, then South-weft, and fouth-weft, and by South 4. oz 5. miles, then fouth-weft and by weft 3. miles, and then South-weft and by Weft 3. miles, and after that weft fouth-weft and South-weft and by fouth 3. miles, till the 7. of Auguft.

The 7. of Auguft till Noone they failed 3. miles weft fouth-weft, then 3. Miles weft, and then they wound South-ward till Euening, and failed 3. miles South-eaft and South-eaft and by eaft, then againe weft fouth-weft, 2. Miles, after that they failed South 3. Miles, till the 8. of Auguft in the Mozning, with a Weft South-weft winde.

The 8. of Auguft they failed South-eaft and by South 10. Miles, and then South-eaft and by Eaft vntill Euening 5. Miles, and then came to a low flat land, that lay fouth-weft and by South, and Nozth-eaft and by Nozth, and fo failed 5. Miles moze, and there they had 36. fadome deepe, 2. Miles from the land, the ground blacke fand; There they failed towards the land, till they were at 12. fadome, and halfe a Mile from the land it was Stony ground.

From thence the land reacheth fouth-ward foz 3. miles, to the other low point that had a blacke Rocke lying close by it, and from thence the land reacheth South fouth-eaft 3. miles, to another point; and there lay a little low Iſland from the point, and within halfe a mile of the land it was flat ground, at 8. 9. and 10. fadome deepe, which they called the black Iſland, becaule it ſhewed blacke aboue, then it was very miſtie, fo that they lay in the wind, and failed 3. Miles Weft Nozth-weft, but when it cleared vp, they wound towards the land againe, and the Sunne being South, they came right againft the Blacke Iſland, and had held their course Eaft South-eaft.

There W. Barents tooke the height of the ſunne it being vnder 71. degrees and ⅓, and there they found a great Creeke, which William Barents iudged to be the place where Oliuer Brunel had beene befoze,

D   called

called Costincsarth.

From the Blacke Island, they sailed South, and South and by east to another small point 3. miles, on which point there stood a Crosse, and therefore they called it the Crosse-point, there also there was a flat Bay, and low water, 5.6.or 7. fadome deep, soft ground.

From Crosse-point they sailed along by the land South South-east 4. Miles, and then came to another small point, which behinde it had a great Creeke, that reached East-ward: This point they called the fifth-point or S.Laurence point. From the fifth point they sailed to the Sconce point 3.Miles, South south-east, and there lay a long blacke Rocke close by the land, whereon there stood a Crosse; then they entered into the Ice againe, and put inward to the Sea because of the Ice. Their intent was to saile along the coast of Noua Zembla to the Wey-gates, but by reason that the Ice met them, they wound West-ward, and from the 9. of August in the Euening, till the 10. of August in the Morning, sayled West and by North 11. Miles, and after that 4. miles west north-west, and North-west and by west, the winde being North; in the Morning they wound East-ward againe, and sailed vntill Euening 10. Miles East and east and by south; after that east and east and by north 4.Miles, and there they saw land, and were right against a great Creeke, where with their boat they went on land, and there found a faire Hauen 5. fadome deepe, sandy ground. This Creeke on the North-side hath 3.blacke points, and about the 3. points lyeth the road, but you must keepe somewhat from the 3. point, for it is stonie, and betweene the 2. and 3.point there is another faire Bay, for North-west, North; and North-east winds, blacke san-dy ground. This Bay they called S. Laurence Bay, and there they tooke the height of the Sunne, which was 70. degrees and ¼.

From S.Laurence Bay, south south-east 2. miles to Sconce point, there lay a long blacke rocke, close by the land, whereon there stood a Crosse, there they went on land with their boat, & perceiued that some men had bin there, and that they were fled to saue themselues, for there they found 6. Sacks with Rie-meale buried in the ground, and a heap of stones by the Crosse, and a bullet for a great piece, and there abouts also there stood another Crosse, with 3. houses made of wood, after the North-countrey manner: and in the houses they found many barrels of Pike-staues, whereby they coniectured, that there they vsed to take Salmons, and by them stood 5, or 6. Coffins, by graues, with dead mens

mens bones, the Coffins ſtanding vpon the ground all filled vp with ſtones; there alſo lay a bꝛoken Ruſſia ſhip, the Keele thereof being 44. foot long, but they could ſee no man on the land: it is a faire Hauen foꝛ all winds, which they called the Meale-hauen, becauſe of the Meale that they found there.

From the blacke Rocke oꝛ Cliffe with the Croſſe, 2. Miles South ſouth-eaſt there lay a low Iſland, a little into the Sea; from whence they ſailed 9. oꝛ 10. Miles South ſouth-eaſt, there the height of the Sunne was 70. degrees and 50. minutes, when it was South ſouth-weſt.

From that Iſland they ſailed along by the land 4. miles South-eaſt and by South, there they came to 2. Iſlands, whereof the vttermoſt lay a mile from the land: thoſe Iſlands they called S. Clara.

Then they entered into the Ice againe, and wound inward to ſea, in the wind, and ſailed from the Iſland vntill Euening Weſt South-weſt 4. Miles, the wind being Noꝛth-weſt; that Euening it was very miſtie, and then they had 80. fadom deepe.

Then againe they ſailed South-weſt and by Weſt, and Weſt South-weſt, 3. Miles, there they had 70. fadome deepe, and ſo ſay-led till the thirteenth of Auguſt in the Moꝛning, South Weſt and by Weſt foure Miles, two houres befoꝛe they had ground at fiftie ſixe Fadome, and in the Moꝛning at foꝛtie fiue Fadome, ſoft muddy ground.

Then they ſayled till Noone ſixe Miles South-weſt, and had twentie foure Fadome deepe, blacke ſandie ground, and within one houre after, they had two and twentie Fadome deepe, bꝛowne reddiſh ſand; then they ſailed ſixe Miles South-weſt, with fifteene fadome deepe, red ſand: after that two Miles South-weſt, and there it was fifteene Fadome deepe, red ſand, and there they ſawe land and ſayled foꝛward South-weſt vntill Euening, till wee were within halfe a mile of the land, and there it was ſeuen fadome deepe, ſandy ground, the land, being low flat Downes reaching Eaſt and Weſt.

Then they wound from the land, and ſailed Noꝛth, and Noꝛth and by Eaſt 4. miles, from thence they wound to land againe, and ſayled til the 14. of Auguſt 5. oꝛ 6. miles ſouth-weſt, ſailing cloſe by the land, which (as they geſſe) was the Iſland of Colgoyen, there they ſailed by the land eaſt-ward 4. miles; after that 3. miles eaſt, & eaſt & by ſouth,

then

then the weather became miftie, whereby they could not fee the land,
and had fhallow flat water at 7. o2 8. fadome; then they tooke in the
Marfaile and lay in the wind, till it was cleare weather againe, and
then the Sunne was South south-weft, yet they could not fee the
land: there they had 100. fadome deepe, fand y ground, then they failed
Eaft 7. miles; after that againe 2. miles Eaft south-eaft, and South-
eaft and by eaft, & againe till the 15. of Auguft in the mo2ning, 9. miles
Eaft south-eaft, then from mo2ning till noone they failed 4. Miles eaft
south-eaft, and failed ouer a flat o2 land, of 9. o2 10. fadome deepe, fan-
dy ground, but could fee no land, and about an houre befo2e noone it
began to ware deeper, fo2 then wee had 12. and 13. fadome water, and
then wee fapled Eaft south-eaft 3. miles, till the Sunne was South-
weft.

The fame day the funne being south-weft, William Barents tooke
the height thereof, and found it to be eleuated aboue the Ho2izon 35.
degrees, his declination being 14. degrees and $\frac{1}{4}$ fo $\dot{y}$ as there wanted
55. degrees of 90. which 55. and 14. Degrees and $\frac{1}{4}$ being both added
together, made 69. degrees 15. minutes, which was the height of the
Pole in that place, the winde being No2th-weft, then they failed 2.
Miles mo2e Eaft-ward, and came to the Iflands called Matfloe and
Delgoy, and there in the mo2ning they meet with the other fhippes
of their company, being of Zelandt and Enck-huyfen, that came out
of Wey-gates the fame day, there they fhewed each other where they
had bin, and how farre each of them had failed, and difcouered.

The fhip of Enck-huyfen had paft the Staights of Wey-gates,
and faid, that at the end of Wey-gates he had found a large fea, and that
they had failed 50. o2 60. Miles further Eaft-ward, and were of
opinion that they had been about the riuer of Obi, that commeth out of
Tartaria, & that the land of Tartaria reacheth no2th-eaft-ward againe
from thence, whereby they thought that they were not far from Cape
Tabin, which is $\dot{y}$ point of Tartaria, that reacheth towards the king-
dom of Chathai, No2th-eaft and then south-ward, and fo thinking
that they had difcouered inough fo2 that time, & that it was too late in
the yeare to faile any further, as alfo that their Commiffion was to
difcouer the fcituation, and to come home againe befo2e winter, they
turned againe towards the Wei-gates, and came to an Ifland about 5.
Miles great, lying south-eaft from Wei-gates on the Tartarian fide,
and called it the States Ifland, there they found many Stones, that
were

were of a Criſtale Mountaine being a kind of Diamont.

When they were met together as I ſayd befoꝛe, they made ſignes of ioy, diſcharging ſome of their oꝛdinance, and were merry, the other ſhippes thinking that William Barents had ſailed round about Noua Zembla, & had come backe againe thꝛough the Wei-gates: & after they had ſhewed each other what they had done, and made ſignes of ioy foꝛ their meeting, they ſet their courſe to turne backe againe foꝛ Holland, and vpon the 16. of Auguſt they went vnder the Iſlands of Matfloc and Delgoy, and put into the road, becauſe the wind was noꝛth-weſt, and lay there till the 18. of Auguſt.

The 18. of Auguſt they ſet ſaile, and went foꝛward Weſt noꝛth-weſt, and almoſt Weſt and by Noꝛth, and ſo ſailed 12. miles, and then weſt and by ſouth 6. Miles, and came to a ſand of ſcarce 5. fadome deepe, with a noꝛth-weſt wind, and in the euening they wound noꝛthward and ſailed Eaſt noꝛth-eaſt 7. oꝛ 8. miles, the wind being noꝛtherly, & then they wound Weſt-ward & ſailed till the 19. of Auguſt in the moꝛning weſt 2. miles, then 2. miles ſouth-weſt, and after that 2. miles ſouth-eaſt: there they wound Weſt-ward againe, and ſailed till Euening with a calme, and after that had an Eaſt winde, and at firſt ſailed Weſt noꝛth-weſt, and Noꝛth-weſt and by weſt 6. oꝛ 7. Miles, and had ground at 12. fadome: then till the 20. of Auguſt in the moꝛning, they ſailed Weſt noꝛth-weſt, and noꝛth-weſt and by Weſt, 7. miles with an Eaſterly wind, & then againe ſailed Weſt noꝛth-weſt, and Noꝛth-weſt and by Weſt 7. miles, then Weſt noꝛth-weſt 4. Miles, and draue foꝛward till euening with a calme: after that they ſailed Weſt noꝛth-weſt and Noꝛth-weſt and by weſt 7. Miles, and in the night time came to a ſand of 3. fadome deepe right againſt the land, and ſo ſailed along by it, firſt one mile Noꝛth, then 3. Miles Noꝛth noꝛth-weſt, and it was ſandy hilly land, and many points: and then ſailed on foꝛward with 9. oꝛ 10. fadome deepe, along by the land, till noone, being the 21. of Auguſt, Noꝛth-weſt 5. Miles; and the Weſt point of the land, called Candinaes, lay noꝛth-weſt from them 4. Miles.

From thence they ſailed 4. Miles Noꝛth noꝛth-weſt, and then noꝛth-weſt and by Noꝛth 4. Miles, and 3. Miles moꝛe Noꝛth-weſt, and noꝛth-weſt & by Noꝛth, and then Noꝛth-weſt 4. Miles, til the 22. of Auguſt in the Moꝛning: and that moꝛning they ſailed Noꝛth-weſt 7. miles, & ſo till euening, weſt noꝛth-weſt & noꝛth-weſt & by weſt 15. miles, the wind being noꝛth, after that 8. miles moꝛe weſt noꝛth-weſt,

D 3

and

and then till the 23. of August at Noone, West north-west 11.miles, the same day at noone the Sunne was eleuated aboue the Horizon 31. Degrees and ⅓ part, his declination was 11.Degrees and ⅔ partes; so that it wanted 58. Degrees and ⅓ of 90. Degrees, and adding the declination being 11. Degrees ⅓ to 58. Degrees, and ⅓ partes, then the height of the Pole was 70. Degrees and ⅓ part : then they sailed North-west, and north-west and by west, till Euening 8.miles, and then North-west and by west, and West north-west 5.Miles, and then vntill the 24. of August in the Morning, North-west, and by west 6.miles, after that West, and West south-west, 3. Miles, and then past close by the Island of Ware-huysen in the roade. From Ware-huysen hither-ward because the way is well knowne, I neede not to write thereof, but that from thence they sailed altogether home-ward, and kept company together till they came to the Texel, where the ship of Zelandt past by, and William Barents with his Pinnace, came vpon a faire day, being the 16. of September before Amster-dam, and the ship of Enck-huysen, to Enck-huysen, from whence they were set foorth. William Barents men brought a Sea-horse to Amsterdam, being of a wonderfull greatnesse, which they tooke vp-on a flake of Ice, and killed it.

The end of his Voiage.

A Briefe Declaration of

a Second Nauigation made in Anno
1595. Behinde *Norway*, *Muscouia*,
and *Tartaria*, towards the King-
doms of *Cathaia* and *China.*

HE 4. ſhips aforeſaid being returned home
about Harueſt-time, in Anno 1594. they
were in good hope that the Voiage aforeſaid
would be done, by paſſing along through the
Straights of Weygates, and ſpecially by the
report made by the 2. ſhips of Zelandt, and
Enck-huyſen, wherein Iohn Huyghen of
Linſchoten was committed, who declared
the manner of their trauell in ſuch ſort, that
the Generall States and Prince Maurice reſolued, in the beginning of
the next yeare to prepare certaine ſhips, not only (as they went before)
to diſcouer the paſſage, but to ſend certaine wares and Merchandiſes
thither, wherein the Marchants might lade what wares they would,
with certaine Factors to ſell the ſaide wares, in ſuch places as they
ſhould arriue, neither paying fraight nor cuſtome. Peter Plantins a
learned Coſmographer being a great furtherer and ſetter forward of
this Voiage, and was their chiefe inſtructer therein, ſetting downe
the ſcituation of the Coaſts of Tartaria, Cathaia, and China; but
how they lye, it is not yet ſufficiently diſcouered, for that the courſes and rules by him ſet downe, were not fully effected, by meanes of
ſome inconueniences that fell out, which by reaſon of the ſhortneſſe of
time could not be holpen. The reaſons that ſome men (not greatly af-
fected to this Voyage) vſe to propound, to affirme it not poſſible to be
done; are taken (as they ſay) out of ſome old & auncient Writers: which
is, ý 350. miles at the leaſt of the north Pole on both ſides are not to be
ſailed

sailed, which appeareth not to be true, for that the white Sea, and far-
ther North-ward, is now sayled & daily fisht in, cleane contrary to the
writings and opinions of auncient Writers; yea, & how many places
hath bin discouered that were not knowne in times past? It is also no
marueile (as in the beginning of the first description of this Voyage I
haue sayd) that vnder the North Pole for 23. degrees, it is as cold on
both sides, one as the other, although it hath not beene fully discouered. Who would beleeue that in the Periudan Mountaines, and the
Alpes that lye betweene Spaine, Italie, Germanie, and France, there
is so great cold, that the Snow thereon neuer melteth, and yet lye
a great deale neerer the Sunne, then the Countries lying on the
North-Seas doe, being low Countries; by what meanes then is it
so cold in those Hilles? onely by meanes of the deepe Vallies wherein the Snow lyes so deepe, that the Sunne cannot shine vpon the
ground, by reason that the high Hilles keepe the Sunne from shining
on them. So it is (as I iudge) with the Ice in the Tartarian seas,
which is also called the Ice-sea, about Noua Zembla, where the Ice
that commeth into those seas out of the Riuers that are in Tartaria
and Cathaia, can not melt, by reason of the great quantitie thereof,
and for that the sun sheweth not high aboue those places, & therefore
casteth not so great a heat, as it can easily melt : which is the cause
that the Ice lyeth there still, as the Snowe doth in the Hilles of
Spaine aforesayd, and that the sayd Ice maketh it farre colder
there, then it is a great deale neerer the Pole in the large seas,
and although those places that are not discouered, cannot bee so
well described, as if they were discouered : yet I thought good to
say thus much for a memoriall; and now I will proceed to the declaration of the second Voyage made into the North-seas.

In Anno 1595. The generall States of the vnited Prouinces, and Prince Maurice, caused seuen shippes to bee prepared to sayle through the Wey-gates or the Staights of Nassaue,
to the Kingdome of Cathaia and China : Two out of Amsterdam,
two out of Zelandt, two out of Enck-huysen, and one out of
Roterdam : sixe of them laden with diuers kindes of Wares,
Marchandizes, and with Money, and Factors to sell the said wares;
the seuenth beeing a Pinace, that had Commission, when the other
shippes were past about the Cape de Tabin (which is the furthest
point of Tartaria) or so farre that they might saile foorth South-
ward

The Nauigation into the North-feas.

ward, without any let oz hinderance of the Ice, to turne backe againe, and to bzing Newes thereof: and I being in William Barents ship, that was our chiefe Pilote, and Iames Hemf-kerke chiefe Factoz, thought good to wzite downe the same in ozder, as it is here after declared, as I did the first Uoyage, accozding to the course and stretching of the land as it lyeth.

First, after we had been muftered at Amfterdam, and euery man taken an oath, that was then purpofely miniftered vnto vs; vpon the 18. of June wee failed to the Texel, from thence to put to sea with other ships that were appointed to meet vs at a certaine day; & so to begin our Uoiage in the Name of God.

The 2. of July wee set saile out of the Texel, in the Mozning at bzeake of day, holding our course Nozth west and by Nozth, and sayled about sixe miles.

After that wee sailed Nozth nozth-west 18. miles, till the 3. of July in the Mozning, being then as wee efteemed vnder 55. Degrees, then the wind being Nozth-weft, and Nozth nozth-weft, calme weather, wee failed Weft, and Weft and by South 4. Miles, till the 4. of July in the Mozning : after that the winde being Nozth nozth-weft, and rather moze Noztherly, wee sayled Weft, and weft and by Nozth 15. Miles, till the 5. of July in the Mozning, and after that 8. Miles moze till the Sunne was weft.

Then we wound about and sailed 10. Miles Nozth-eaft, till the 6. of July in the Mozning, and so held on our course foz the space of 24. miles till the 7. of July, the Sunne being South, and held the same course foz 8. Miles, till mid-night.

Then wee wound about and failed Weft south-weft fourteene Miles, till the ninth of July in the Mozning, and then againe wee wound Nozth Eaft-ward, till Euening and so sayled about tenne Miles.

And then eighteene Miles moze eaft-ward, till the tenth of July in the Euening; then we wound about againe and sailed South-weft, eight Miles, till the 11. of July, the Sunne then being South-Eaft.

Then wee wound Nozth, and Nozth and by Eaft, about sixteene Miles, till the twelue of July, and then Nozth and by Weft tenne miles.

The 13. of July wee wound about againe, and sailed South-

E   weft

weſt, and Weſt South-weſt 10. Miles, till about three houres before Euening : then wee wound againe, and ſailed North north-eaſt 10. Miles, till the 14. of July, the Sunne being South South-eaſt, and then North and by Eaſt, and North north-eaſt 18. Miles, till the 15. of July in the Morning : after that North and by Eaſt 12. miles, vntill Euening, then wee ſaw Norway : and then wee ſayled North and by Eaſt 18. Miles, till the 16. of July in the Euening ; at that time the Sunne being North-weſt, and vpon the 17. of July, North-eaſt, and North-eaſt and by North, 24. Miles, till the ſunne was in the Weſt.

Then againe we ſayled north-eaſt 20. miles, till the 18. of July, the Sunne being North-weſt, from thence wee ſayled North-weſt, and by North 18. Miles, till the 19. of July, when the Sunne was weſt.

From thence againe we wound about; North-eaſt and by North, and North-eaſt till the 20. of July, while ſixe Glaſſes were run out, in the firſt quarter, and then ſtayed for our Pinnace, that could not follow vs, becauſe the wind blew ſo ſtiffe: that quarter being out, we ſaw our company lying to Lee-ward, to ſtay for vs, and when wee were gotten to them, wee helde our courſe (as before) till Euening, and ſailed about 30. Miles.

Then we ſayled South-eaſt and by Eaſt 26. Miles, till the 21. of July in the Euening, when wee let our watch, and held on the ſame courſe for 10. miles till the 22. of July, the ſun being South south-eaſt, the ſame euening the ſun being south south-weſt we ſaw a great Whale, right before our bough, that lay and ſlept, which by the ruſhing of the ſhip that made towards it, and the noyſe of our men awaked, and ſwamme away, or els wee muſt haue ſailed full vpon her, and ſo wee ſayled eight Miles, till the Sunne was North North-weſt.

The thirteenth of July wee ſayled South-eaſt and by South fifteene Miles, till the ſunne was South South-weſt, and ſaw land about foure Miles from vs, Then wee wound of from the Land, when the Sunne was about South South-weſt, and ſayled twentie foure Miles till Euening, that the Sunne was North-weſt.

After that we ſayled North-ward tenne Miles, till the fifteenth of July, at Noone, and then North North-weſt eight Miles till Mid-night, then wee wound about againe, and ſayled Eaſt, South-eaſt, and South-eaſt and by South, till the twentie ſixe of July, the

Sunne

Sunne being South, and had the Sunne at seauentie one Degrees and ¼.

The Sunne beeing South South-west, wee wounde about againe, and sayled North-east and by North, till the Seauen and twentie of July, the Sunne being South; being vnder 72. degrees and ⅓. partes.

After that, wee sayled full North-east 16. Myles, till the 28. of July, the Sunne being East. Then we wound about againe South and by East, till the Sunne was North-west, and sayled 8. Miles. After that, South-east and by South 18. Miles, till the 19. of July at midnight.

After that, we wound about againe, East and by North, and sayled eight miles, till the 30. of July, when the Sunne was North: then we wound South south-east, with caime weather, till the 31. of July, that the Sunne was North-west, and sayled sixe Miles.

From thence wee sayled East-ward 8. Myles, till the first of August about midnight, in calme faire weather, and saw Trumpsand South-east from vs, the Sunne being North: and wee being tenne Miles from the land, and so sayled till the Sunne was East, with a litle cold gale out of the East North-east, and after that, South-east 9. Myles and a halfe, till the Sunne was North-west.

Then we wound about againe, being halfe a Mile from the land, and sayled East and by North three miles, till the 3. of August, the Sunne South-west: and then along by the land about 5. Miles.

Then we wound about againe, because there lay a Rocke or Sand, that reached about a mile and a halfe out from the land into the Sea, whereon Isbrant the Uize-admirall stroke with his Shippe: but the weather being faire and good, he got off againe. When he stroke vpon it, he was a litle before vs; and when we heard him cry out, and saw his Shippe in danger, wee in all haste wound about; & the Wind being North-east and by East, and South-east and South-east and by South, wee sayled 5 or 6. Myles along by the land, till the Sunne was South, vpon the 4. of August.

Then we tooke the height of the Sunne, and found it to be Seauentie and one degrees and ¼. At which time till noone, wee had calme weather: and hauing the Wind Southerly wee sayled East and by North, till the sixth of August, the Sunne being South-east,

E 2   the

the North Cape lying about two miles, East from vs, and when the Sunne was North-west, the mother and her daughters lay South-ward from vs foure miles, and in that time we sailed about fourteene miles.

Then we sailed East north-east, till the 6. of August, when wee had the Sunne West north-west, and then Is-brandt the Uize-admi-rall, came to vs with his ship, and so bating some of our saples, wee sayled about 10. miles.

Then we hoysed vp our sailes againe, till the Sunne was North-west, and after that halde vp againe with an East, and East-northeast wind, and sailed south and by west with a stiffe gale, till the 7. of August, that the Sunne was south-east, then their came a ship of Enck-huysen out of the white sea, and then we esteemed that wee had sailed about 8. Miles.

The Sunne being south, the North Cape lay south-west and by south from vs, about a mile and a halfe, and the mother and her daugh-ters south-west from vs, about 3. miles, then hauing an East and by north wind we wound about, and held our course North and by east, and sailed 14. miles till the 8. of August, when the Sunne was south-west; then we wound south and by east, and so held her course till the 9. of August, that the sunne was south; and then we saw a high point of land south-east from vs, and another high point of land south-ward, about 4. miles from vs, as we gesse, and so we sailed about 14. miles : and then againe we wound North-east, & by North, till the 10. of August, the sun being east, and sailed about 8. miles; after that we wound south-ward againe, till the sunne was North-west, and sailed (as we gesse) 10. miles.

Then wee wound about againe, when the North Cape lay West and by south from vs about 9. Miles, the North-kyen being South and by West from vs, about 3. Miles, and sailed North north-east till the 11. of August, in very mistie weather 10. miles, till the sunne was south.

From thence wee wound about againe, with an East North-east wind, and sailed south-east and by south 8. Miles, till the sunne was south-west, vpon the 12. of August, then the North-kyen lying south west and by south from vs about 8. miles, we lay and draue at sea, in calme weather, till the 13. of August, when the sunne was south south-west, and in that time sailed about 4. miles.

Then

Then we failed south-east and by east, about 4. Glasses, and then the Iron-hogge, with her companie (being Marchants) tooke their course south-ward, and wee failed till the 14. of August (when the sunne was south) about 18. miles, and from thence for the most part, held one course till the 15. of August, the sunne being East, and there we cast out the lead and found 70. fadome deepe, and sailed 38. Miles till the sunne was south.

The sunne being south and the height thereof being taken, it was found to be 70. Degrees and 47. minutes, then in the night time wee cast out the lead, & found ground at 40. fadome, it being a bancke, the sunne being North-west, we cast out the lead againe and had ground at 64. fadome, and so wee went on East south east till the 16. of August, the sunne being North-east, & there the line being out, we found no ground at 80. fadome, and after that we sailed East and east, and by south, and in that time wee cast the lead often times out, and found ground at 60. and 70. Fadome either more or lesse, and so sailed 36. Miles, till the sunne was south.

Then we sailed East, and so continued till the 17. of August, the sunne being east, and cast out our lead, and found 60. Fadome deepe, clay ground, and then taking the height of the sunne, when it was south-west and by south, we found it to be 69. Degrees and 54. Minutes, and there we saw great store of Ice, all along the coast of Noua Zembla, and casting out the lead had 75. fadome soft ground, and so sayled about 24. miles.

After that we held diuers courses because of the Ice, and sayled south-east and by east, and south south-east, for the space of 18. miles, till the 18. of August, when the Sunne was East, and then wee cast out the lead againe, and found 30. fadome soft ground, and within 2. houres after that 25. fadome, red sand, with small shels : Three glasses after that we had ground at 20. fadome, red sand, with blacke shels, as before : then we saw 2. Islands, which they of Enck-huysen gaue the names of Prince Maurice and his brother, which lay from vs south-east 3. miles, being low land, and then we sailed 8. miles, till the Sunne was South.

Then we sailed East, and oftentimes casting out the lead we found 20. 19. 18. and 17. fadome deepe, good ground mixed with blacke shels, and saw the Wey-gates (the Sunne being west) which lay east north-east from vs about 5. miles, and after that we sailed about 8. miles.

Then

Then we sailed vnder 70. Degrees, vntill we came to the Wey-gates, most part through broken Ice, and when we got to Wey-gates, we cast out our lead, and for a long time found 13. and 14. fadome, soft ground, mixed with blacke shels, not long after that wee cast out the lead and found 10. fadome deepe, the wind being North, and wee forced to hold stifly aloofe, in regard of the great quantitie of Ice, till about midnight, then we were forced to wind North-ward, because of certaine rocks that lay on the South-side of Wey-gates, right before vs, about a mile and a halfe, hauing ten fadome deepe : then wee changed our course, and sailed West North-west for the space of 4. Glasses, after that we wound about againe East, and East and by South, and so entred into Wey-gates, and as wee went in, we cast out the lead, and found 7. fadome deepe little more or lesse, till the 19. of August, and then the sunne being South-east, we entered into the Wey-gates, in the road, the Wind being North.

The right Chanell betweene the Image point and the Samuters land was full of Ice, so that it was not weil to be past through, and so we went into the road (which wee called the Trayen Bay, because we found store of Trayen-oyle there, this is a good bay for the course of the Ice, and good almost for all Windes, and we may saile so farre into it as we will, at 4. 5. & 3. fadome, good anchor-ground, on the East side it is deepe water.

The 20. of August, the height of the Sunne being taken with the Crosse-staffe, wee found that it was eleuated aboue the Horizon 69. Degrees 21. minuts, when it was South-west and by South, being at the highest, or before it began to descend.

The 21 of August we went on land with in the Wey-gates with foure and fiftie men, to see the situation of the Countrey, and being 2. miles within the land, we found many Vel-werck, Trayen, and such like wares, and diuers foot-steps of men, and Deere; whereby wee perceiued that some men dwelt thereabouts, or else vsed to come thither.

And to assure vs the more thereof, wee might perceiue it by the great number of Images, which wee found there vpon the Image or Beelthooke (so called by vs) in great aboundance, whereof ten dayes after we were better informed by the Samuters and the Russians, when we spake with them.

And

And when wee entered further into the Land, wee vsed all the meanes we could, to see if we could finde any houses, o2 men, by whom wee might bee info2med of the scituation of the Sea there abouts, whereof afterward wee had better intelligence by the Samuters; that tolde vs, that there are certaine men dwelling on the Wey-gates, and vpon NouaZembla, but wee could neither finde men, houses, no2 any other things, so that to haue better info2mation, we went with some of our men further South-east into the land; towards the Sea side; and as we went, we found a path-way made with mens feete in the Mosse o2 Marsh-ground, about halfe knee deepe, fo2 that going so deepe wee felt hard ground vnder our feete, which at the deepest was no higher then our shoes, and as wee went fo2-ward to the Sea Coast, wee were exceeding glad, thinking that wee had seene a passage open, where wee might get th2ough, because we saw so little Ice there: and in the Euening entering into our ship againe, wee shewed them that newes. Meane time our Maister had sent out a boat to see if the Tartarian Sea was open, but it could not get into the Sea because of the Ice, yet they rowed to the Crosse-point, and there let the Boate lye, and went ouer the Land to the West point, and there perceiued that the Ice in the Tartarian Sea, lay full vpon the Russian Coastes, and in the mouth of Wey-gates.

The twentie th2ee of August wee found a Lodgie, o2 Boate of Pitzo2e, which was sowed together with bast o2 ropes, that had beene No2th-ward to seeke fo2 some Sea-ho2ses teeth, Trayen, and Geete, which they fetcht with their Boat, to lade in certaine shippes that were to come out of Russia, th2ough Wey-gates.

Which shippes they sayd (when they spake with vs) were to saile into the Tartarian Sea, by the Riuer of Oby, to a place called Vgolita in Tartaria, there to stay all Winter, as they vsed to doe euery yeere: and told vs that it would yet bee nine o2 tenne Weekes ere it began to Freeze in that place, and that when it once began to freeze, it would freeze so hard, that as then men might goe ouer the Sea into Tartaria, (along vpon the Ice) which they cal-led Mermare.

The 24. of August in the Mo2ning betimes, we went on board of the Lodgie, to haue further info2mation and instruction of the Sea,

on

on the East side of Wey-gates, and they gaue vs good instruction, such as you haue heard.

The 25. of August we went againe to the Lodgie, and in friendly maner spake with them, we for our parts offering them friendship; and then they gaue vs 8. fat Geese, that lay in the bottome of their Boat: we desired that one or two of them would goe with vs on board our ship, and they willingly went with vs to the number of seuen; and being in our ship they wondered much at the greatnesse, and furniture of our ship: and after they had seene and looked into it in euery place, we set Fish, Butter, and Cheese before them to eat, but they refused it; saying, that that day was a fasting day with them, but at last when they saw some of our pickled-Herrings, they eat them both heads, tayles, skin, and guts, and hauing eaten thereof, we gaue them a small ferkin of Herrings, for the which they gaue vs great thankes, knowing not what friendship they should doe vs to requite our courtesie, and wee brought them with our Pinnace into the Traen Bay.

About Noone wee hoysed vp our anchors with a West north-west wind; the course or stretching of Wey-gates, is east to the Cruis point, and then North-east to the Twist point, & somewhat more Easterly: From thence the land of Wey-gates reacheth North north-east, and North and by East, and then North, and somewhat westerly, we sayled North-east and East-ward 2. miles, by the Twist point, but then we were compelled to saile backe againe, because of the great store of Ice, and tooke our course to our road aforesaid: and sayling backe againe wee found a good place by the Crosse point to anchor in, that night.

The 26. of August in the Morning we hoysed anchor, and put out our fork-saile, and so sailed to our old road, there to stay for a more conuenient time.

The 28. 29. and 30. of August till the 31. the winde for the most part was South-west, and William Barents our Captaine, sayled to the Southside of Wey-gates, and there went on land, where wee found certaine Wilde men (called Samuters) and yet not altogether wilde, for they being 20. in number staid & spake with our men, being but 9. together, about a mile within the land, our men not thinking to find any men there (for that we had at other times beene on land in the Wey-gates, and saw none) at last it being mistie weather, they perceiued men, fiue and fiue in a company, and wee were hard by them

before

Wey-gates, and saw none) at last, it being mistie weather, they perceiued men 5. and 5. in a company, and wee were hard by them before
we knew it : then our Interpretor went alone towards them to speake
with them; which they perceiuing, sent one towardes vs, who comming almost to our men, tooke an Arrow out of his quiuer, offering to
shoote at him; wherewith our Interpretor, being without Armes,
was afraide, and cryed vnto him, saying (in Russian speach;) Shoote
not, we are friends: which the other hearing, cast his Bow and Ar-
rowes to the ground, therewith giuing him to vnderstand that he was
well content to speake with our man: which done, our man called to
him once againe, and sayd: Wee are friendes: whereunto he made answere & sayd; then you are welcome: and saluting one the other, ben-
ded both their heades downe towardes the ground, after the Russian
manner: this done, our Interpretor questioned with him, about the
scituation & stretching of the Sea eastward through the Straightes of
Wey-gates; whereof he gaue vs good instruction, saying: that when
they should haue past a poynt of Land about 5. dayes sayling from
thence, shewing North-eastward;) that after that, there is a great
Sea (shewing towardes the South-east vpward,) saying, that hee
knew it very well, for that one had been there that was sent thither by
their King with certaine Souldiers, whereof he had been Captaine.

The maner of their Apparell is, like as we vse to paint Wild men,
but they are not wilde; for they are of reasonable iudgement: they
are apparelled in Hartes skins from the head to the feete, vnlesse it
be the principallest of them, which are apparelled, whether they bee
men or women, like vnto the rest, as aforesayd, vnlesse it bee on their
heads, which they couer with certaine coloured Cloth lyned with
Furre the rest weare Cappes of Hartes or Buckes skinnes, the
rough side outwardes, which stand close to their heades, and are very
fitte. They weare long Hayre, which they plaite and fold, and let it
hang downe vpon their backes. They are (for the most part all) short
and low of stature, with broad flat faces, small eyes, short legges, their
knees standing outwards; and are very quicke to goe and leape.
They trust not Strangers; for although that wee shewed them all
the courtesie and friendship that wee could, yet they trusted vs not
much: which we perceiued hereby, that as vpon the first of September we went againe on land to them, and that one of our men desired

to see one of their Bowes: they refused it, making a signe that they would not doe it. Hee that they called their King, had Centinels standing abroad, to see what was done in the Countrie, and what was bought and sould: At last, one of our men went neerer to one of the Centinels, to speake with him, and offered him great friendship, according to their accustomed manner, withall giuing him a Bisket; which he with great thankes tooke, and presently eate it; and while he eate it, hee still lookt diligently about him on all sides what was done.

Their Sleades stood alwayes ready with one or two Hartes in them, that runne so swiftly with one or two men in them, that our Horses are not able to follow them. One of our men shot a Musket towards the Sea, wherewith they were in so great feare, that they ranne and leapt like mad men: yet at last, they satisfied themselues, when they perceiued that it was not maliciously done to hurt them: and we told them by our Interpretor, that wee vsed our Peeces in stead of Bowes; whereat they wondered, because of the great blow and noyse that it gaue and made: and to shew them what we could doe therewith, one of our men tooke a flatte Stone about halfe a handfull broad, and set it vpon a Hill a good way off from him: which they perceiuing, and thinking that wee meant some-what thereby, 50. or 60. of them gathered round about vs; and yet some-what farre off, wherewith hee that had the Peece, shotte it off, and with the Bullet smote the Stone in sunder: whereat they woondred much more then before.

After that, we tooke our leaues one of the other, with great friendship on both sides; and when we were in our Penace, we al put off our Hattes, and bowed our Heades vnto them, sounding our Trumpet: They (in their manner) saluting vs also, & then went to their Sleads againe.

And after they were gone from vs, and were some-what within the Land, one of them came ryding to the shore, to fetch a rough-heawed Image, that our men had take off the shore, & caryed into their Boate: And when he was in our Boate, and perceiued the Image, hee made vs a signe that wee had not done well to take away that Image: Which wee beholding, gaue it to him againe: Which when he had receiued, he placed it vpon a hill right by the sea side, and tooke

it

it not with him, but sent a Slead to fetch it from thence: and as farre as wee could perceiue, they esteemed that Image to be their God; for that right ouer against that place in the Wey-gates, which wee called Beelchooke, wee found certaine hundreds of such carued Images, all rough about the Heads, being somewhat round, and in the middle hauing a litle hill in stead of a Nose; and about the Nose two cuttes, in place of Eyes; and vnder the Nose a cutte, in place of a Mouth. Before the Images, wee found great store of Ashes, and Bones of Hartes: whereby it is to be supposed, that there they offered vnto them.

Hauing left the Samuters, the Sunne being South-ward, William Barents our Captaine, spake to the Admirall to will him to set sayle, that they might goe forward: but they had not so many wordes togeather, as was betweene them the day before; for that when the Admirall and Uize-admirall had spoken with him, the Admirall seeming to be well contented therewith, said vnto him: Captaine, What thinke you were best for vs to doe? He made answere. I thinke wee should doe well to set sayle, and goe forward on our Uoyage, that wee may accomplish it. Whereunto the Admirall answeared him, and sayd. Looke well what you doe Captaine: at which time, the Sunne was North-west.

The 2. of September a litle before Sunne rising, wee put foorth our Anckor to get out, for that the Winde as then blew South south-west; it being good weather to get out, and ill weather to lie still: for we lay vnder a low Bancke. The Admirall and Uize-admirall, seeing vs making out, began also to hoyse their Anckors, and to set sayle.

When wee put out our Focke-sayle, the Sunne was East and by South: and then we sayled to the Crosse-poynt, and there wee cast Anckor to stay for the Uize-admirals Pinnace; which with much labour and paines, in time got out of the Ice, by often casting out of their Anckor: and in the euening shee got to vs: in the morning about 2. houres before Sunne rising, we set sayle, and by Sunne rising, we got within a mile East-ward of the Twist-poynt, and sayled North-ward 6. miles, till the Sunne was Souh. Then wee were forced to wind about, because of the great quantitie of Ice, and the Mist that then fell, at which time the Winde blew so vncertaine,

F 2   that

that we could hold no course, but were forced continually to winde and turne about, by reason of the Ice, and the vnconstantnesse of the wind, together with the mist, so that our course was vncertaine, and we supposed that we had sailed south-ward vp towardes the Samuters countrey, and then held our course south-west, till the watchers were northwest from vs; then we came to the point of the States Island, lying East-ward about a musket shot from the land, hauing 13. fadome deepe.

The 4. of September, we hoysed anchor, because of the Ice, and sailed betweene the firme land and the States Island, where wee lay close by the States Island at 4. and 5. fadome deepe, and made our shippe fast with a cable cast on the shoare, & there we were safe from the course of the Ice, and diuers time went on land, to get Hares whereof there were many in that Island.

The 6. of September, some of our men went on shore vpon the firme land to seeke for stones, which are a kinde of Diamont, whereof there are many also in the States Island: & while they were seeking ye stones, 2. of our men lying together in one place, a great leane white beare came sodainly stealing out, and caught one of them fast by the necke, who not knowing what it was that tooke him by the necke, cried out and said; Who is that that pulles me so by the necke? wherewith the other that lay not farre from him; lifted vp his head to see who it was, and perceiuing it to be a monsterous beare, cryed and sayd, Oh Mate it is a Beare, and therewith presently rose vp and ran away.

The Beare at the first faling vpon the man, bit his head in sunder, and suckt out his blood, werewith the rest of the men that were on land, being about 20. in number, ran presently thither, either to saue the man, or else to driue the beare from the dead body: and hauing charged their peeces and bent their pikes set vpon her, that still was deuouring the man, but perceiuing them to come towardes her, fiercely and cruelly ran at them, and gat another of them out from the companie which she tare in peeces, wherewith all the rest ran away.

We perceiuing out of our ship and Pinace that our men ran to the sea-side to saue themselues, with all speed entered into our Boates, and rowed as fast as we could to the shoare to relieue our men. Where being on land, we beheld the cruell spectacle of our two dead men, that had beene so cruelly killed and torne in peeces by the Beare, wee seeing

that

that incouraged our men to goe backe againe with vs, and with pee-ces, curtelaxes, and halfe-pikes to set vpon the Beare, but they would not all agree thereunto : some of them saying, our men are already dead, and we shall get the Beare well enough, though wee oppose not our selues into so open danger, if wee might saue our fellowes liues, then we would make haste, but now wee neede not make such speede, but take her at an aduantage, with most securitie for our selues, for we haue to doe with a cruell fierce and rauenous beast. Whereupon three of our men went forward, the Beare still deuouring her prey, not once fearing the number of our men, and yet they were thirtie at the least : the three that went forward in that sort, were Cornelius Ia-cobson, Maister of William Barents shippe, William Gysen, Pilote of the Pinace, and Hans van Nufflen, William Barents Purser : and after that the sayd Maister and Pilote had shot three times, and miss, the Purser stepping somewhat further forward, and seeing the Beare to be within the length of a shot, presently leauelled his peece, and discharging it at the Beare, shot her into the head, betweene both the eyes, and yet shee held the man still fast by the necke, and lifted vp her head, with the man in her mouth, but shee beganne somewhat to stagger, wherewith the Purser and a Scotishman, drew out their courtlaxes, and stroke at her so hard, that their Courtlaxes burst, and yet she would not leaue the man, at last William Geysen went to them, and with all his might stroke the Beare vpon the snowt with his peece, at which time the Beare fell to the ground, making a great noyse, and William Geyson leaping vpon her cut her throat. The seuenth of September wee buryed the dead bodyes of our men in the States Iland, and hauing fleaed the Beare, carryed her skinne to Amsterdam.

The ninth of September, wee set saile from the States Is-land, but the Ice came in so thicke and with such force, that wee could not get through, so that at Euening wee came backe againe to the States island, the winde being Westerly. There the Admirale and the Pinace of Roterdam, fell on ground by certaine rockes, but gote off againe without any hurt.

The tenth of September, wee sayled againe from the States Is-land, towards the Weygates, and sent two Boates into the Sea, to certifie vs what store of Ice was abroad : and that Euening we came

all

all together into Wey-gates, and anckored by the Twift point.

The 11. of September in the Morning, we failed againe into the Tartarian sea, but we fell into great store of Ice, so that wee failed backe againe to the Wey-gates, & anckored by the Crosse point, and about mid-night we saw a Russian Lodgie, that failed from the Beelt-point towardes the Samuters Land. The 13. of September, the Sunne being South, there beganne a great storme to blowe out of the South South-west, the weather being mistie, melancholly, and snowie, and the storme increasing more and more we draue through.

The 14. of September the weather beganne to bee somewhat clearer, the winde being North-west, and the Storme blowing stiffe out of the Tartarian Sea, but at Euening it was faire weather, and then the winde blewe North-east, the same day our men went on the other side of Wey-gates, on the firme land, to take the depth of the channell, and entered into the bough behinde the Islands, where there stood a little howse made of wood, and a great fall of water into the land. The same Morning wee hoysed vp our anchor, thinking once againe to try what we could doe to further our Voyage, but our Admirall being of another minde, lay still till the fifteene of September.

The same day in the Morning, the winde draue in from the East end of the Wey-gates, whereby wee were forced presently to hoyse anchors, and the same day sailed out from the West ende of the Wey-gates, with all our Fleete, and made home-wardes againe, and that day past by the Islands called Matfloe and Delgoy, and that Night wee sayled twelue Miles, North-west and by West, till Saterday in the Morning, and then the winde fell North-east, and it began to snow.

The 16. of September, from Morning to Euening, wee sayled West North-west 18. Miles, at 42. Fadome deepe, in the night it snowed & there blew very much winde out of the North-east: the first quarter wee had 40. Fadome deepe, but in the Morning we saw not any of our ships.

After that wee sailed all the night againe, till the 17. of September in the Morning, with two schower sailes, North-west: and by West, and West North-west 10. Miles, the same day in the second quarter we had 50. Fadome deepe, and in the Morning 38.

Fadome

Fadome deepe, sandy ground with blacke shels.

Sunday in the Morning wee had the winde North, and North North-west with a great gale, and then the Admirals Pinnace kept vs company, and sailed by vs with one saile from Morning to Euening, South South-west, and South-west and by South, for the space of 6. Miles.

Then wee saw the point of Candynaes, lying South-east from vs, and then wee had 27. Fadome deepe, redde sand with blacke shels. Sunday at night wee put out our focke sayle, and wound North-ward ouer, and sayled all that night till Munday in the Morning, 7. or 8. Miles North-east, and North-east and by East.

The 18. of September in the Morning, wee lost the sight of the Pinnace that followed vs, and till Noone sought after her, but wee could not finde her, and sailed East-ward 3. Miles, and from Noone till Night, wee sailed North and by East foure Miles. And from Munday at night, till Tuesday in the Morning, North-east and by North, seuen Miles, and from Morning till Noone, North-east and by North 4. Miles: and from Noone till night, North-east 5. or 6. Miles at 55. Fadome deepe, the same Euening wee woond South-ward and sailed so till Morning.

The 20. of September, wee sayled South and by West, and South South-west 7. or 8. Miles, at 80. fadome deepe, blacke slimie ground; from Morning till Noone, wee sailed with both our Marsh sailes, South-west, and by West 5. Miles, and from Noone to night, West and by South 5. Miles.

The 21. of September from night, till thursday in the morning, wee sayled one quarter West, and so till day still West 7. miles at 64. fadome deepe, oasie ground.

From Morning till noone south-west 5. Miles at 65. fadome deepe Oasie ground : at noone wee wound North-ward againe, and for three houres, sayled North-east two Myles : then we wound West-ward againe, and sayled till night, while halfe our second quarter was out, with two Schoure sayles south south-west, and southwest and by south sixe myples. After that, in the second quarter, wee wound North-ward, and sayled so till Fryday in the morning.

The 22. of September, wee sayled North and by East, and North

North-

The Nauigation into the North-seas.

North-east 4. miles, and from morning till noone, North-east 4.
Myles. Then we wound West-ward againe, and sayled North-west
and by West, and North-west three Miles: After that, the first quarter North-west and by West fiue miles: The second quarter, West
and by North foure miles, and till Saterday in the morning, being
the 23. of September, West South-west, and South-west and by
West foure miles: From Saterday in the morning till euening, wee
sayles with two Schoure sailes South-west and South-west and by
West 7. or 8. miles, the Winde being North North-west. In the
Euening we wound North-ward, and sayled till Sunday in the morning, being the 24. of September, with two Schoure sayles, very
neare East, with a stiffe North North-west Wind 8. miles; and from
morning till noone East and by South three miles, with a North
Winde: Then we wound West-ward, and till euening sayled West
South-west three miles; and all that night, till Monday in the morning: The 25. of September, West and by South sixe miles, the
Winde being North. In the morning the Winde fell North-east,
and we sailed from morning till euening West, and West & by North
10. miles hauing 63. Fadome deepe sandy ground.

From Euening till Tuesday in the Morning, being the 26. of
September, we sailed West 10. Miles, and then in the Morning wee
were hard by the land, about 3. Miles East-ward from Kildwin, and
then we wound off from the land, and so held off for 3. houres together,
after that we wound towards the land againe, and thought to goe into
Kilduin, but we were too low, so that after-noone we wound off from
the land againe, and till Euening sailed East North-east 5. Miles,
and from Euening til two houres before Wednesday in the Morning,
being the 27. of September, we sailed East 6. Miles, then we wound
West-ward, and till Euening sailed West and by North 8. Miles,
and in the Euening came againe before Kilduin, then wee wound
farre off from the land, and sailed 2. quarters North-east and by East,
and East North-east 6. Miles, and about Friday in the Morning,
being the 28. of September wee wound about againe, and sayled
with diuers variable Windes, sometimes one way, then another
way till Euening, then wee gest that Kilduin lay West from vs
foure Miles, and at that time wee had an East North-east Winde,
and

and fayled North North-West, and North-West and by North, till Satterday in the Morning 12. or 13. Miles.

The nine and twenteeth of September in the Morning, wee fayled North-West, and by West foure Miles, and all that day till Euening it was faire, still, pleasant, and Sunne-shine Weather. In the Euening wee went West South-West, and then wee were about sixe Miles from the land, and fayled till Sunday in the Morning, beeing the 30. of September, North North-West eight Miles, then wee wound towardes the Land, and the same day in the Euening entered into Ward-house, and there wee stayed till the tenth of October. And that day wee set fayle out of Ward-house, and vpon the eighteene of Nouember, wee arriued in the Maes.

The course or Miles from Ward-house into Holland, I haue not here set downe, as being needlesse, because it is a continuall Voiage knowne to most men.

The end of the second Voyage.

G   The

The third Voyage North-
ward to the Kingdomes of *Cathaia*, and
China, in Anno 1596.

FTER that the seuen Shippes (as I
saide before) were returned backe againe
rom their North Uoiage, with lesse bene-
ât then was expected, the Generall States
of the vnited Prouinces consulted together, to send certaine ships thither againe,
a third time, to see if they might bring the
sayd Uopage to a good end, if it were
possible to bee done: but after much con-
sultation had, they could not agree there-
on; yet they were content to cause a Proclamation to be made, that if
any either Townes or Marchants, were disposed to venture to make
further search that way, at their owne charges, if the Uopage were
accomplished, and that thereby it might bee made apparant, that the
sayd passage was to be sayled, they were content to giue them a good
reward, in the Countryes behalfe, naming a certaine summe of money. Whereupon in the beginning of this yeare, there was two
ships rigged, and set foorth by the Towne of Amsterdam, to sayle
that Uopage, the men therein being taken vp vpon two conditions:
viz: What they should haue if the Uopage were not accomplished,
and what they should haue if they got through, and brought the Uoiage to an end, promising them a good reward if they could effect it,
thereby to incourage the men, taking vp as many vnmarryed men
as they could, that they might not bee disswaded by meanes of their
wiues and children, to leaue off the Uopage. Upon these conditions,
those two shippes were ready to set saile in the beginning of May.

In

In the one, Iacob Heemskerke Hendrickson , was Master and Factor for the Wares and Marchandiſes ; and William Barents chiefe Pilote. In the other Iohn Cornelison Rijp, was both Maſter and Factor for the goods that the Marchants had laden in her.

The 5. of May all the men in both the ſhippes were muſtered, and vpon the tenth of May they ſayled from Amſterdam, and the 13. of May got to the Vlie. The ſixteenth wee ſet ſaile out of the Vlie, but the tyde being all moſt ſpent, and the winde North-eaſt, we were compelled to put in againe, at which time, Iohn Corneliſons ſhip fell on ground, but got off againe, and wee anchored at the Eaſt ende of the Vlie. The 18. of May wee put out of the Vlie againe, with a North-eaſt winde, and ſayled North North-weſt. The 22. of May wee ſaw the Iſlands of Hitland, and Feyerd-land, the winde beeing North-eaſt. The 24. of May, wee had a good winde, and ſayled North-eaſt, till the 29. of May : then the Winde was againſt vs, and blewe North-eaſt in our Top-ſayle. The 30. of May we had a good Winde, and ſailed North-eaſt, and we tooke the heigth of the ſunne with our Croſſe-ſtaffe, and found that it was eleuated aboue the Horizon 47. Degrees and 42. Minutes, his declination was 21. Degrees and 42. Minutes. ſo that the height of the Pole was 69. Degrees and twentie foure Minutes.

The firſt of June wee had no night, and the ſecond of June wee had the Winde contrary, but vpon the fourth of June, wee had a good winde, out of the Weſt North-weſt, and ſayled North-eaſt.

And when the Sunne was about South South-eaſt, wee ſaw a ſtrange ſight in the Element : for on each ſide of the Sunne there was another Sunne, and two Raine-bowes that paſt cleane through the three Sunnes, and then two Raine-bowes more, the one compaſſing round about the Sunnes, and the other croſſe through the great run-dle ; the great rundle ſtanding with the vttermoſt point, eleuated a-boue the Horizon 28. Degrees : at Noone the Sunne beeing at the higheſt, the height thereof was meaſured, and wee found by the Aſtrolabium, that it was eleuated aboue the Horizon 48. Degrees, and 43. Minutes, his declination was 22. Degrees and 17. Minutes, the which beeing added to 48. Degrees 43. Minutes, it was found that wee were vnder 71. Degrees of the height of the Pole.

Iohn

Iohn Cornelis shippe held aloofe from vs, and would not keepe with vs, but wee made towardes him, and sayled North-east, bating a point of our Compasse, for wee thought that wee were too farre West-ward, as after it appeared, otherwise wee should haue held our course North-east. And in the Euening when wee were together, wee tolde him that wee were best to keepe more Easterly, because wee were too farre West-ward, but his Pilote made answere, that they desired not to goe into the Straights of Weygates. There course was North-east and by North, and wee were about 60. Miles to Sea-warde in from the Land, and were to sayle North-east, when wee had the North Cape in sight, and therefore wee should rather haue sailed East North-east, and not North North-east, because wee were so farre West-ward, to put our selues in our right course againe: and there wee tolde them, that wee should rather haue sayled East-ward, at the least for certaine Miles, vntill wee had gotten into our right course againe, which by meanes of the contrary Winde wee had lost; as also because it was North-east: but whatsoeuer wee sayde, and sought to councell them for the best, they would holde no course but North North-east, for they alleaged, that if wee went any more Easterly, that then wee should enter into the Wey-gates, but wee being not able to perswade them, altered our course one point of the Compasse, to meete them, and sayled North-east and by North, and should otherwise haue sayled north-east, and somewhat more East.

The fifth of June wee sawe the first Ice, which wee wondered at, at the first, thinking that it had beene white Swannes, for one of our men walking in the Fore-decke, on a suddaine beganne to cry out with a loude voyce, and sayd; that hee sawe white Swans: which wee that were vnder Hatches hearing, presently came vp, and perceiued that it was Ice, that came driuing from the great heape, showing like Swannes, it being then about Euening, at mid-night, wee sailed through it, and the Sunne was about a Degree eleuated aboue the Horizon in the North.

The sixth of June, about foure of the Clocke in the afternoone, wee entred againe into the Ice, which was so strong that wee could not passe through it, and sayled South-west, and by West, till eight Glasses were runne out, after that wee kept on our course North,

North-

North-east, and sayled along by the Ice.

The seuenth of June wee tooke the height of the Sunne, and found that it was eleuated aboue the Horizon thirtie eight Degrees and thirtie eight Minutes, his declination beeing twentie two Degrees thirtie eight Minutes; which beeing taken from thirtie eight Degrees thirtie eight Minutes, wee found the Pole to bee seuentie foure Degrees; there wee found so great store of Ice, that it was admirable: and wee sayled along through it, as if wee had past betweene two Lands. The water being as greene as grasse, and wee supposed that we were not farre from Greene-land, and the longer wee sayled the more and thicker Ice we found.

The eight of June, wee came to so great a heape of Ice, that wee could not saile through it, because it was so thicke, and therefore wee wound about South-west and by West, till two Glasses were runne out, and after that three Glasses more South South-west, and then South three Glasses, to sayle to the Island that wee saw, as also to shunne the Ice.

The ninth of June wee found the Islande, that lay vnder 74. Degrees and 30. Minutes, and as wee gest, it was about fiue miles long.

The tenth of June wee put out our Boate, and therewith eight of our men went on Land, and as wee past by Iohn Cornelisons shippe, eight of his men also, came into our Boate, whereof one was the Pilote. Then William Barents asked him, whether wee were not too much West-ward, but hee would not acknowledge it: whereupon there passed many wordes betweene them, for William Barents sayde hee would prooue it to bee so, as in trueth it was.

The eleuenth of June going on Land, wee found great store of Sea-Mewes Egges vpon the shoare, and in that Island, wee were in great danger of our liues: for that going vp a great Hill of Snowe, when we should come downe againe, wee thought wee should all haue broken our neckes, it was so slipperie, but wee sate vpon the Snowe, and slidde downe, which was very dangerous for vs, to breake both our armes and legges, for that at the foote of the Hill there was many Rockes, which wee were likely to haue fallen vpon, yet by Gods help wee got safely downe againe.

Meane

Meane time William Barents sate in the Boate, and sawe vs slide downe, and was in greater feare then wee, to behold vs in that danger. In the sayd Island wee found the varying of our Compasse, which was 13. Degrees, so that it differed a whole point at the least: after that wee rowed aboard Iohn Cornelisons shippe, and there wee eate our Eggs.

The 12. of June in the morning, wee saw a white Beare, which wee rowed after with our Boate, thinking to cast a Roape about her neike; but when we were neere her, shee was so great, that wee durst not doe it, but rowed backe againe to our Shippe to fetch more men and our Armes, and so made to her againe with Muskets, Hargubushes, Halbertes, and Hatchets. Iohn Cornelysons men comming also with their Boate to helpe vs : and so beeing well furnished of Men and Weapons, wee rowed with both our Boates vnto the Beare, and fought with her while foure Glasses were runne out, for our Weapons could doe her litle hurt : and amongst the rest of the blowes that wee gaue her, one of our men stroke her into the backe with an Axe, which stucke fast in her backe, and yet she swomme away with it; but wee rowed after her, and at last wee cut her head in sunder with an Axe, wherewith she dyed : and then wee brought her into Iohn Cornelysons Shippe, where wee fleaed her, and found her Skinne to bee twelue foote long : which done, wee eate some of her flesh; but wee brookt it not well. This Island wee called the Beare-Island.

The 13. of June, we left the Island, and sayled North, and somewhat Easterly, the Winde being West and South-west, and made good way : so that when the Sunne was North, wee gest that wee had sayled 16 miles North-ward from that Island.

The 14. of June, when the Sunne was North, wee cast out our Lead 113. Fadome deepe, but found no ground, and so sayled forward till the 15. of June, when the Sunne was South-east with mistie and misling weather, and sayled North and North and by East : about Euening it cleared vp, and then wee saw a great thing vtuing in the Sea, which wee thought had been a Shippe : but passing along by it, wee perceiued it to be a dead Whale, that stouncke monsterously; and on it there sate a great number of Sea-meawes : At that time, we had sayled 20. miles.

The

The 16. of June, with the like speede wee sayled North and by East, with mistie weather; and as we sayled, wee heard the Ice before wee saw it: but after, when it cleared vp, wee saw it, and then wound off from it, when as wee guest wee had sayled 30. miles.

The 17. and 18. of June, wee saw great store of Ice, aud sayled a-long by it, vntill wee came to the poynt, which we could not reach, for that the Winde was South-east, which was right against vs, and the poynt of Ice lay South-ward from vs : yet we laueared a great while to get beyond it, but we could not do it.

The 19. of June we saw Land againe, then wee tooke the height of the Sunne, and found that it was eleuated aboue the Horizon 33. degrees and 37. minutes : her declination being 23. degrees and 26. minutes ; which taken from the sayd 33. degrees and 37. minutes, we found that we were vnder 80. degrees and 11. minutes : which was the height of the Pole there.

This Land was very great, and we sayled West-ward along by it, till wee were vnder 79. degrees and a halfe, where we found a good road, and could not get neare to the Land, because the Winde blew North-east, which was right off from the Land : the Bay reacht right North and South, into the Sea.

The 21. of June we cast out our Anchor, at 18. Fadome before the Land; and then wee, and Iohn Cornelysons men, rowed on the West side of the Land, and there fetcht Balast : and when wee got on Board againe with our Balast, wee saw a white Beare that swamme towardes our Shippe; wherevpon we left off our worke, and ente-ring into the Boate with Iohn Cornelisons men, rowed after her, and crossing her in the way, droue her from the Land, where-with shee swamme further into the Sea, and wee followed her; and for that our Boate could not make good way after her, we manned out our Scute also, the better to follow her : but shee swamme a mile into the Sea; yet wee followed her with the most part of all our men of both shippes in three Boates, and stroke often times at her, cutting and heawing her, so that all our Armes were most broken in peeces. During our fight with her, shee stroke her Clowes so hard in our Boate, that the signes thereof were seene in it; but as hap was, it was in the forehead of our Boate : for if it had been in the middle thereof, shee had (perad-uenture) euer throwne it, they haue such force in their Clawes :

At

The Nauigation into the North-seas.

At laſt, after we had fought long with her, and made her wearie with our three Boates that kept about her, wee ouercame her, and killed her: which done, we brought her into our ſhippe, and ſleaed her: her ſkinne being 13. foote long.

After that, we rowed with our Scute, about a mile inward to the Land, where there was a good Hauen, and good Anchor ground, on the Eaſt-ſide being ſandie, there wee caſt out our Leade, and found 16. Fadome deepe, and after that 10.and 12. Fadom, and rowing further, we found that on the Eaſt-ſide there was two Iſlands, that reached Eaſt-ward into the Sea: on the Weſt-ſide alſo there was a great Creeke or Riuer, which ſhewed alſo like an Iſland. Then we rowed to the Iſland that lay in the middle, and there we found many red Geeſe-Egges, which we ſaw ſitting vpon their Neſts, and draue them from them, and they flying away, cryed, red, red, red: and as they ſate wee killed one Gooſe dead with a ſtone, which we dreſt and eate, and at leaſt 60. Egges, that we tooke with vs aboard the ſhippe, and vpon the 22.of June, wee went aboard our ſhippe againe.

Thoſe Geeſe were of a perfit red coulor, ſuch as come into Holland about Weiringen, and euery yeere are there taken in aboundance, but till this time it was neuer knowne where they hatcht their Egges, ſo that ſome men haue taken vpon them to write, that they ſit vpon trees in Scotland, that hang ouer the Water, and ſuch Egges as fall from them downe into the Water, become yong Geeſe, and ſwimme there out of the Water; but thoſe that fall vpon the Land burſt in ſunder, and are loſt: but this is now found to be contrary, and it is not to bee wondered at, that no man could tell where they breed their Egges, for that no man that euer we knew, had euer beene vnder 80. degrees: nor that Land vnder 80. Degrees, was neuer ſet downe in any Card, much leſſe the red Geeſe that breed therein.

Red Geeſe breed their yong Geeſe, vnder 80. Degrees in Green-land.

Note.

It is here alſo to be noted, that although that in this land which we eſteeme to be Greene-land, lying vnder 80.Degrees,and more, there groweth leaues and graſſe,and that there are ſuch beaſts therein as eat graſſe,as Harts, Buckes and ſuch like Beaſtes as liue thereon, yet in Noua Zembla, vnder 76.Degrees, there groweth neither leaues nor graſſe, nor any beaſts that eate graſſe or leaues, liue therein; but ſuch beaſts as eate fleſh, as Beares and Foxes: and yet this Land lyeth full 4.Degrees from the North-pole, as Greene-land aforeſaid doth.

The

The 23. of June we hoyfted Anchor againe, and fayled North-weft-ward into the fea; but could get no further, by reafon of the Ice; and fo wee came to the fame place againe where wee had laine, and caft Anchor at 18. Fadome: and at Euening being at Anchor, the Sunne being North-eaft, and fomewhat more Eaft-warde, wee tooke the height thereof, and found it to be eleuated aboue the Horizon 13. degrees and 10. minutes; his declination being 23. degrees and 28. minutes: which fubftracted from the height aforefaid, refteth 10. degrees and 18. minutes, which being fubftracted from 90. degrees, then the height of the Pole there was 79. degrees and 42. minutes.

After that, wee hoyfted Anchor againe, and fayled along by the Weft fide of the Land, and then our men went on Land, to fee how much the needle of the Compaffe varyed: Meane time, there came a great white Beare fwimming towardes the Shippe, and would haue climbed vp into it, if we had not made a noyfe; and with that we fhot at her with a Peece, but fhe left the Shippe, and fwam to the Land, where our men were: which wee perceiuing, fayled with our Shippe towardes the Land, and gaue a great fhoute; wherewith our men thought that wee had fallen on a Rocke with our Shippe, which made them much abafhed; and therewith the beare alfo being afraide, fwam off againe from the Land, and left our men, which made vs gladde: for our men had no Weapons about them.

Touching the varying of the Compaffe, for the which caufe our men went on Land, to try the certaintie thereof: it was found to differ 16. degrees.

The 24. of June we had a South-weft Winde, and could not get aboue the Ifland, and therefore wee fayled backe againe, and found a Hauen that lay foure Myles from the other Hauen, on the Weft fide of the great Hauen, and there caft Anchor at twelue Fadome deepe: there wee rowed a great way in, and went on Land; and there wee founde two Sea-horfes Teeth that waighed fixe pound: Wee alfo found many fmall Teeth, and fo rowed on board againe.

The 25. of June wee hoyfted Anchor againe, and fayled along by the Land, and went South, and South South-weft, with a

H.   North

North North-east Winde, vnder 79. Degrees. There we found a great Creeke oz Riuer, whereinto we sailed ten miles at the least, holding our course South-ward; but we perceiued that there wee could not get through: there wee cast out our Leade, and foz the most part found ten sadome deepe, but wee were constrained to lauere out againe, foz the Winde was Northerly, and almost full North, and wee perceaued that it reached to the firme Land, which we supposed to be Low-land, foz that wee could not see it any thing farre, and therefoze wee sailed so neere vnto it, till that wee might see it, and then we were forced to lauere, and vpon the 27. of June we got out againe.

The twenty eight of June, wee gate beyonde the point that lay on the west-side, where there was so great a number of Birds, that they flew against our sailes, and we sailed 10. Miles South-ward, and after that West, to shun the Jce.

The twenty nine of June wee sapled South-East and somewhat moze Easterly, along by the land, till wee were vnder 76. degrees and 50. Minutes, foz wee were forced to put off from the land, because of the Jce.

The thirteeth of June, we sapled South, and somewhat east, and then we tooke the height of the Sunne, and found that it was eleuated aboue the Hozizon 38. Degrees and 20. Minutes, his declination was 23. Degrees and 20. Minutes, which being taken from the fozmer height, it was found that wee were vnder 75. Degrees.

The first of July, wee saw the Beare-Island againe, and then Iohn Cornelison and his Officers came aboard our ship, to speake with vs about altering of our course, but wee being of a contrary opinion, it was agreed that wee should follow on our course, and hee his: which was, that hee (accozding to his desire) should saile vnto 80. Degrees againe: foz hee was of opinion, that there hee should finde a passage through, on the East-side of the Land, that lay vnder 80. Degrees. And vpon that agreement wee left each other, they sayling North-ward, and wee South-ward, because of the Jce, the Winde being East South-east.

The second of July, wee sailed East-ward, and were vnder 74. Degrees, hauing the Winde North North-West, and then wee
wound

wound ouer another Bough, with an East North-east Winde, and sayled North-ward. In the Euening the Sunne beeing about North-West, and by North, wee wound about againe, (because of the Ice) with an East Winde, and sailed South South-east, and about East South-east, and then we wound about againe (because of the Ice) and the Sunne being South south-West, we wound about againe, and sailed North-east.

The third of July, wee were vnder 74. Degrees, hauing a South-east and by East Wind, and sailed north-east and by north: after that we wound about againe with a South Winde, and sayled East South-east, till the sunne was North-West, then the Wind began to be somewhat larger.

The fourth of July, wee sailed East and by North, and found no Ice, which wee wondered at, because wee sailed so high, but when the Sunne was almost South, we were forced to winde about againe, by reason of the Ice, and sailed West-ward, with a North Wind, after that the Sunne beeing North, wee sailed East South-east, with a North-east Wind.

The fifth of July, wee sailed North North-east, till the Sunne was South: then wee wound about, and went East South-east, with a North-east Winde. Then wee tooke the height of the Sunne, and found it to bee eleuated aboue the Horizon 39. Degrees 27. Minutes, his declination beeing 22. Degrees and 53. Minutes, which taken from the high aforesaid, we found that wee were vnder the height of the Poole seuentie three Degrees and 20. Minutes.

The seuenth of July, wee cast out our whole Lead-lyne, but found no ground, and sayled East and by South, the Wind being North-east and by East, and were vnder 72. Degrees and 12. Minutes.

The eight of July, we had a good North-west Wind, and sailed East and by North, with an indifferent cold gale of Wind, and got vnder 72. Degrees and 15. Minutes. The ninth of July, we went East and by North, the Wind being West. The tenth of July, the Sunne being South south-West, we cast out our Lead, and had ground at 160. Fadome, the Winde being North-east, and by North, and we sailed East and by South, vnder 72. Degrees.

The

The 11. of July, we found 70. Fadome deepe, and saw no Jce, then we gest that we were right South, and North from Dandinaes, that is the East-point of the White-Sea, that lay Southward from vs, and had sandy ground, and the Bancke stretched North-ward into the Sea, so that wee were out of doubt that we were vpon the Bancke of the White Sea, for wee had found no sandy ground all the Coast along, but onely that Bancke. Then the winde being East and by South, we sayled South, and South and by East, vnder 72. Degrees, and after that, we had a South South-East Winde, and sayled North-East to get ouer the Bancke.

In the Morning wee draue forward with a calme, and found that wee were vnder 72. Degrees, and then againe wee had an East South-east Winde, the Sunne beeing about South-west, and sayled North-east, and casting out our Lead found 150. Fadome deepe clay ground; and then we were ouer the Bancke, which was very narrow, for wee sailed but 14. Glasses, and gate ouer it, when the sunne was about North North-east.

The twelfth of July, wee sayled North and by East, the Winde beeing East, and at Euening the Sunne being North North-east, we wound about againe, hauing the Winde North North-east, and sayled East and by South, till our first quarter was out.

The thirteenth of July, wee sayled East, with a North North-east Winde: then wee tooke the height of the Sunne, and found it to bee eleuated aboue the Horizon 54. Degrees and 38. Minutes, his declination was 21. Degrees and 54. Minutes, which taken from the height aforesaid, the height of the Pole was found to be 73. Degrees, and then againe wee found Jce, but not very much, and wee were of opinion that wee were by Willoughbies-land.

The fourteenth of July wee sayled North-east, the Winde being North North-west, and in that sort sayled about a dinner time, along through the Jce, and in the middle thereof wee cast out our leade, and had 90. Fadome deepe, in the next quarter wee cast out the Leade againe, and had 100. Fadome deepe, and we sayled so farre into the Jce, that wee could goe no further: for wee

could

could see no place where it opened, but were forced (with great labour and paine) to luere out of it againe, the Winde blowing West, and wee were then vnder seuentie foure Degrees and tenne Minutes.

The fifteenth of July wee draue through the middle of the Ice with a calme, and casting out our Leade had 100. Fadome deepe, at which time the Winde being East, wee sayled West.

The sixteenth of July wee got out of the Ice, and sawe a great Beare lying vpon it, that leaped into the Water when shee saw vs: Wee made towards her with our shippe, which shee perceiuing gotte vp vpon the Ice againe, wherewith wee shot once at her.

Then we sailed East South-east, and saw no Ice, gessing that wee were not farre from Noua Zembla, because wee saw the Beare there vpon the Ice, at which time we cast out the Lead and found 100. fadome deepe.

The seuenteenth of July, wee tooke the height of the sunne, and it was eleuated aboue the Horizon 37. Degrees, and 55. Minutes, his declination was 21. Degrees and 15. Minutes, which taken from the height aforesaid. the heigh of the Pole was 74. Degrees and 40. Minutes: and when the Sunne was in the South, wee saw the Land of Noua Zembla, which was about Lomsbay: I was the first that espied it. Then wee altered our course, and sayled North-east and by North, and hopsed vp all our sailes, except the Fore-saile and the Lesien.

The eighteenth of July wee saw the Land againe, beeing vnder 75. Degrees, and sayled North-east and by North, with an North-west Winde, and wee gate aboue the point of the Admirals Island, and sailed East North-east, with a West Winde, the Land reaching North-east, and by North.

The ninteenth of July wee came to the Crosse-Island, and could then get no further, by reason of the Ice, for there the Ice lay still close vpon the Land, at which time the Winde was West, and blewe right vpon the Land, and it lay vnder 76. Degrees and 20. Minutes. There stood 2. Crosses vpon the Land, whereof it had the Name.

The twenteeth of July wee anchored vnder the Island, for wee

wee could get no further for the Ice. There wee put out our
Boate, and with eight men rowed on Land, and went to one of
the Crosses, where we rested vs awhile, to goe to the next Crosse,
but beeing in the way we saw two Beares by the other Crosse,
at which time wee had no weapons at all about vs. The Beares
rose vp vpon their hinder feete to see vs (for they smell further
then they see)and for that they smelt vs:therefore they rose vpright,
and came towards vs,wherewith we were not a little abashed, in
such sort that wee had little lust to laugh, and in all haste went to
our Boate againe, still looking behinde vs, to see if they followed vs,thinking to get into the Boate,and so put off from the land,
but the Master stayed vs, saying, hee that first beginnes to runne
away, I will thrust this Hake-staffe (which hee then held in his
hand) into his Ribs, for it is better for vs (sayd hee) to stay altogether,and see if we can make them afraid with whooping and hal-
lowing, and so wee went softly towardes the Boate, and gote
away glad that wee had escaped there clawes, and that wee had the
leysure to tell our fellowes thereof.

　　The one and twenteeth of July, wee tooke the height of the
Sunne, and found that it was eleuated aboue the Horizon thirtie
fiue Degrees and fifteene Minutes, his declination was one and
twentie Degrees, which being taken from the height aforesaide,
there rested fourteene Degrees, which substracted from ninetie
Degrees,then the heigh of the Pole was found to bee seuentie sixe
Degrees and fifteene Minutes, then wee found the variation of the
Compasse to be iust twentie sixe Degrees. The same day two of
our men went againe to the Crosse, and found no Beares to trouble vs, and wee followed them with our Armes, fearing least wee
might meet any by chance, and when we came to the second Crosse,
wee found the foote-steps of 2. Beares, and saw how long they
had followed vs, which was an hundreth foote-steps at the least,
that way that wee had beene the day before.

　　The two and twentie of July, being Munday, wee set vp
another Crosse, and made our Marke thereon: and lay there before the Crosse Iland, till the fourth of August, meane time we
washt and whited our linnen on the shoare.

　　The thirtie of July, the Sunne being North, there came a
Beare

Beare so neere to our shippe, that wee might hit her with a stone, and wee shot her into the foote with a Peece, wherewith shee ranne halting away.

The one and thirteeth of July, the Sunne being East North-east, seuen of our men killed a beare, and fleaed her, and cast her body into the Sea. The same day at Noone (by our Instrument) wee found the variation of the nedle of the Compasse to be 17. Degrees.

The first of August, wee saw a white Beare, but shee ranne away from vs.

The fourth of August wee got out of the Ice, to the other side of the Island, and anchored there: where, with great labour and much paine, wee fetched a Boate full of stones from the land.

The fifth of August wee set saile againe towardes Ice-point, with an East Wind, and sailed South south-east, and then North North-east, and saw no Ice by the land, by the which wee lauered.

The sixth of August, wee gate about the point of Nassawe, and sayled forward East, and East and by South, along by the land.

The seuenth of August, wee had a West South-west Wind, and sayled along by the Land, South-east, and South-east and by East, and sawe but a little Ice, and then past by the Trust-point, which we had much longed for: at Euening we had an East Wind, with mistie Weather, so that wee were forced to make our ship fast to a peece of Ice, that was at least 36. fadome deepe, vnder the water, and more then 16. fadome aboue the water: which in all was 52. fadome thick, for it lay fast vpon ground the which was 36. fadome deepe. The eight of August in the Morning, wee had an East wind, with mistie Weather.

The 9. of August, lying still fast to the great peece of Ice, it snowed hard, & it was misty weather, and when the sunne was south, we went vpon the Hatches (for we alwayes held watch) where as the Master walked along the ship, he heard a beast snuffe with his nose, and looking ouer-bord, he saw a great beare hard by the ship, where with he cryed out, a Beare, a beare; and with that all our men came vp from vnder hatches, and saw a great beare hard by our boat, seeking to get into it, but we giuing a great shoute shee was afrayd, and

swamme

swamme away, but presently came backe againe, and went behinde a great peece of Ice, whereunto wee had made our Shippe fast, and climbed vpon it, and bouldly came towardes our Shippe to enter into it: but wee had torne our Scute sayle in the Shippe, and lay with foure Peeces before at the Bootesprit, and shotte her into the body: and with that, shee ranne away; but it snowed so fast, that wee could not see whither shee went: but wee guest that shee lay behinde a high Hoouell; whereof there was many vpon the peece of Ice.

The Tenth of August, being Saterday, the Ice began mightily to breake, and then wee first perceiued that the great peece of Ice whereunto wee had made our Shippe fast, lay on the ground; for the rest of the Ice draue along by it, wherewith wee were in great feare that wee should be compassed about with the Ice, and therefore wee vsed all the diligence and meanes that wee could, to get from thence, for wee were in great doubt: and being vnder sayle, wee sayled vpon the Ice, because it was all broken vnder vs, and got to an other peece of Ice; whereunto wee made our Shippe fast againe with our Sheate Anchor, which wee made fast vpon it; and there wee lay till Euening: and when wee had supped, in the first quarter, the sayd peece of Ice began on a sodaine to burst and rende in peeces, so fearefully that it was admirable; for with one great cracke it burst into foure hundred peeces at the least: wee lying fast to it, weied our Cable, & got off from it, vnder the water it was ten Fadome deepe, and lay vpon the ground, and two Fadome aboue the Water; and it made a fearefull noyse both vnder and aboue the Water when it burst, and spread it selfe abroad on all sides.

And being with great feare, gotten from that peece of Ice, wee came to an other peece, that was sixe Fadome deepe vnder the Water: to the which we made a Rope fast on both sides.

Then wee saw an other great peece of Ice, not farre from vs, lying fast in the Sea, that was as sharpe aboue, as it had been a Tower; whereunto wee rowed: and casting out our Lead, wee found that it lay 20. Fadome deepe, fast on the ground vnder the Water, and 12. Fadome aboue the Water.

The

The 11 of August being funday, wée rowed to another péece of Ice, & caſt out our lead,and found that it lay 18 fadom dépe faſt to the ground vnder the water, and 10 fadome aboue the water. The 12 of Auguſt,we ſailed néere vnder the land, ỹ better to ſhun ỹ Ice, foʒ ỹ the great flakes that dʒaue in the ſea, were many fadome dépe vnder the water, and we were better defended from them being at 4.and ʃ fadome water,and there ran a great current of water from the hill. There we made our ſhip faſt againe to a péece of Ice, and called that point, the ſmall Ice point.

The 13 of Auguſt in the moʒning,there came a Beare from the eaſt point of the land, cloſe to our ſhip, and one of our men with a péece, ſhot at her, and bʒake one of her legs, but ſhe crept vp the hill with her thʒée féet,and wée following her,killed her,and hauing ſtead her, bʒought the ſkinne aboard the ſhip. From thence we ſet ſaile, with a little gale of winde, and were foʒced to lauere, but after, that it began to blow moʒe out of the South and South-South-Eaſt.

The 15 of Auguſt, we came to the Iſland of Orange, where we were incloſed with the Ice, hard by a great péece of Ice where we were in great danger to lóſe our ſhip. but with great labour and much paine, we got to the Iſland, the winde being South-Eaſt, whereby we were conſtrained to turne our ſhip, and while we were buſied thereabouts, and made much noiſe, a Beare that lay there and ſlept, awaked, and came towards vs to the ſhip, ſo that we were foʒced to leaue our woʒke about turning of the ſhip, and to defend our ſelues againſt the Beare, and ſhot her into the body, wherewith ſhe ran away to the other ſide of the Iſland,and ſwam into the water, and got vp vpon a péece of Ice, where ſhé lay ſtill, but we comming after her to the péece of Ice where ſhé lay, when ſhe ſaw vs, ſhe leapt into the water, and ſwam to the land. but we got betwéene her and the land. and ſtroke her on the head with a hatchet,but as often as we ſtroke at her with the hatchet, ſhe duckt vnder the water. whereby we had much to do befoʒe we could kill her: after ſhe was dead we ſtead her on the land, and tóoke the ſkin on board with vs,and after that,turned our ſhip to a great péece of Ice, and made it faſt thereunto.

The 16 of Auguſt, ten of our men entring into one boat, rowed to the firme land of Noua Zembla, and dʒew the boate vp

I   vpon

vpon the Ice, which done, we went vp a high hill, to see the fitua-
tion of the land, and found that it reached South Eaft, & South
South Eaft, and then againe South, which we difliked, for that
it lay fo much Southward: but when we faw open water, South
Eaft, and Eaft South Eaft, we were much comforted againe,
thinking ẙ wee had won our voyage, & knew not how wee fhould
get fone inough on boord, to certifie VVilliam Barents thereof.

The 18, of Auguft we made preparation to fet faile, but it was
all in vaine: for we had almoft loft our fheat Anchor, and two new
ropes, and with much loft labour got to the place againe from
whence we came: for the ftreame ran with a mighty currant, and
the Ice draue very ftrongly vpon the cables, along by the fhippe,
fo that we were in feare that we fhould loofe all the cable that was
without the fhip, which was 200. fadome at the leaft, but God
prouided well for vs, fo that in the end, wee got to the place a-
gaine from whence we put out.

The 19. of Auguft it was indifferent good weather, the winde
blowing South weft, the Ice ftill driuing, and we fet faile with
an indifferent gale of wind, and paft by ẙ point of Defire, whereby we were once againe in good hope, and when we had gotten a-
boue the point, we failed South-eaft into the fea-ward, 4. miles,
but then againe we entred into more Ice, whereby we were conftrained to turn back againe, & failed North-weft vntil we came to
ẙ land againe, which reacheth from the point of Defire, to the head
point, south and by weaft 6. miles: from the head point to Fluf-
ingers head, it reacheth South weft, which are 3 miles one from
the other: from the Flufhingars head, it reacheth into the fea, eaft
south eaft, and from Flufhingers head to the point of the Ifland,
it reacheth south weft, and by south, and South weft 3. miles: &
from the Ifland point, to the point of the Ice hauen, the land reacheth Weft South weft 4. miles: from the Ice hauens point to
the fall of water, or the ftreame bay, and the Low land it reacheth
Weft & by South, and Eaft, and by North 7. miles: from thence
the land reacheth Eaft and Weft.

The 21 of Auguft we failed a great way into the Ice hauen,
and that night ankored therein: next day the ftreame going extreame hard Eaftward, we haled out againe from thence, and failed againe to the Ifland point, but for that it was mifty weather,
com-

comming to a péece of Ice, we made the ship fast thereunto, becaufe the winde began to blow hard South weast and South South Welt. There we went vp vpon the Ice, and wondzed much thereat, it was such manner of Ice: Foz on the top it was ful of earth, and there we found aboue 40 Egges, and it was not like other Ice, foz it was of a perfect azure coloure, like to the skies, whereby there grew great contentiõ in wozds amongst our men, some saying that it was Ice, others that it was frozen land: foz it lay vnreafonable high aboue the water, it was at leaft 18. fadome vnder the water close to the ground, and 10. fadome aboue the water. there we ftayed all that ftozme, the wind being Southwest and by Welt.

The 23. of Auguft we failed againe from the Ice, south east-ward into the fea, but entred pzefently into it againe, & wound about to the Ice hauen. The nert day it blew hard Nozth Nozth-welt, and the Ice came mightily dziuing in, whereby we were in a manner compaffed about therewith, and withall the winde be-gan moze and moze to rife, and the Ice ftill dzaue harder and har-der, so that the pin of the rot er and the rother were shozne in péeces and our boate was shozne in péeces betwéene the ship and the Ice, we expecting nothing elfe, but that the ship alfo would be pzeft and crusht in péeces with the Ice.

The 25. of Auguft the weather began to be better, and we toke great paines, and beftowed much labour to get the Ice, where-with we were so inclosed, to go from vs, but what meanes foeuer we vfed it was all in vaine, but when the fun was South-west, the Ice began to dziue out againe with the ftreame, & we thought to faile fouthward about Noua Zembla, to the ftraites of Mer-gates, foz that féeing we could there find no paffage. We hauing paft Noua Zembla, were of opinion that our labour was all in vaine, and that we could not get thzough, and so agréed to go that way home againe; but comming to the ftreame Bay, we were fozced to go back againe, becaufe of the Ice which lay so faft there-abouts, and the fame night also it froze, that we could hardly get thzough there, with the little wind that we had, the winde then being Nozth.

The 26. of Auguft there blew a reafonable gale of winde, at which time we determined to faile back to the point of Defire, &

so home againe, seeing ỹ we could not get through ỹ Wergats, although we vsed al the meanes & industry we could to get forward, but whē we had past by ỹ Ice hauen, ỹ Ice began to driue wͣ such force, ỹ we were inclosed round about therwith, & yet we sought al the meanes we could to get out, but it was all in vaine: and at that time we had like to haue lost three men that were vpon the Ice to make way for the ship, if the Ice had held ỹ course it went, but as we draue back againe, & that the Ice also wheron our men stood, in like sort draue, they being nimble, as ỹ ship draue by thē, one of them caught hould of the beake head, another vpon the shroudes, and the third vpon the great brase that hung out behind, and so by great aduenture by the hold that they toke, they got safe into the shippe againe, for which they thanked GOD with all their hearts: for it was much liklier that they should rather haue béene carried away with the Ice, but God, by the nimblenes of their hands, deliuered them out of that danger which was a pittifull thing to behold, although it fell out for the best, for if they had not béene nimble, they had surely dyed for it.

The same day in the euening, we got to the West side of the Ice hauen, where we were forced in great cold, pouerty, misery, and griefe, to stay all that Winter, the winde then being East-North-east.

The 27 of August the Ice draue round about the ship, and yet it was good wether, at which time we went on land, and being there it began to blow South-east, with a reasonable gale, and then the Ice came with great force before the bough, and draue the ship vp foure foote high before, and behind it séemed as if the kéele lay on the ground, so that it séemed that the ship would be ouerthrowne in the place, whereupon they that were in the ship, put out the boate, therewith to saue their liues, and withall pnt out a flagge to make a signe to vs, to come on board: which we perceiuing, and beholding the ship to be lifted vp in that sort, made all the haste we could to get on board, thinking that the ship was burst in péeces, but comming vnto it, we found it to be in better case then we thought it had béene.

The 28 of August, wée gat some of the Ice from it, and the ship began to sit vpright againe, but before it was fully vpright, as William Barents and the other pilot went forward to the bough

to

to sée how the ship lay, and how much it was risen; and while they were busie vpon their knées and elbowes to measure how much it was, the ship burst out of the Ice with such a noyse and so great a crack, that they thought verely that they were all cast away, knowing not how to saue them selues.

The 29 of August, the ship lying vpright againe, we vsed all the meanes we could, with yron hookes, & other instruments, to breake the flakes of Ice that lay one heap'd vpō the other, but al in vaine; so that we determined to commit our selues to the mercie of God, and to attend ayde from him, for that the Ice draue not away in any such sort that it could helpe vs.

The 30 of August, the Ice began to driue together one vpon the other with greater force then before, and bare against the ship wt a boystrous south-west wind, and a great snowe, so that all the whole ship was borne vp and inclosed, whereby all that was both about it and in it, began to crack, so that it séemed to burst in a 100 péeces, which was most fearfull both to sée and heare and made all ye haire of our heads to rise vpright with feare: & after yt, the ship (by the Ice on both sides that ioyned and got vnder the same) was driuen so vpright, in such sort, as if it had bin lifted vp with a wrench or vice.

The 31 of August, by the force of the Ice, the ship was driuen vp 4 or 5 foote high at the beaks head, and the hinder part thereof lay in a clift of Ice, whereby we thought that the ruther would be fréed from the force of the flakes of Ice, but notwithstanding, it brake in péeces staffe and all: and if that the hinder part of the ship had bin in the Ice that draue, as well as the fore part was then all the ship would haue bin driuen wholly vpon the Ice, or possibly haue ran on groūd, and for that cause wée were in great feare, and set our Scutes and our boate out vpon the Ice, if néede were, to saue our selues, but within 4 houres after, the Ice draue awaye: of it selfe, wherewith we were excéeding glad, as if we had saued onr liues, for that the ship was then on float againe, and vpon that we made a new ruther and a staffe, and hung the ruther out vpon the hooks, that if we chanced to be born vpon the Ice againe, as we had bin, it might so be fréed from it.

The 1. of September being Sunday, while we were at praier, the Ice began to gather together againe, so that the ship was lifted

I 3   vp vp two foote at the leaſt, but the Ice brake not. The ſame euening the Ice continued in ẙ ſort ſtil driuing and gathering together, ſo that we made preparation to draw our Scute and the boate ouer the Ice vpon the land, the wind then blowing South-eaſt.

The ʒ.of September, it ſnowed hard with a North-eaſt wind, & the ſhip began to riſe vp higher vpõ the Ice, at which time the Ice burſt and crakt, with great force, ſo that we were of opinion to carry our Scute on land in that fowle weather with 1 ʒ. barrels of bread, & two hogſheds of wine to ſuſtaine our ſelues if næd were.

The ʒ of Septẽber it blew hard but ſnowed not ſo much, ẙ wind being North Northeaſt, at which time we began to be looſe from the Ice, whereunto we lay faſt, ſo that the Scheck broke fron the Steuen, but the planks wherewith the ſhip was lyned, held the Scheck faſt and made it hang on, but the boutlowce and a new cable if we had fallen vpon the Ice) brake by the forcible preſſing of the Ice, but held faſt againe in the Ice, and yet the ſhip was ſtaunch, which was wonder, in regard ẙ the Ice draue ſo hard, and in great heapes, as big as the ſalt hils that are in Spaine, and within a harquebus ſhot of the ſhip betwæne the which we lay in great feare and anguiſhe.

The 4.of September, the weather began to cleare vp, and we ſawe the Sunne, but it was very cold, the wind being North-eaſt we being forced to lye ſtill.

The 5.of September, it was faire ſunſhine weather and very calme, and at euening when we had ſupt the Ice compaſſed about vs againe, and we were hard incloſed therwith, the ſhip beginning to lye vpon the one ſide, and leakt ſore, but by Gods grace, it became ſtaunch againe, wherewith we were wholly in feare to looſe the ſhip, it was in ſo great danger: at which time we tooke counſell together & caried our old ſock ſaile, with pouder, lead, pæces muſkets & other furniture on land, to make a tent about our Scute, ẙ we had drawẽ vpon the land, & at that time we carried ſome bread and wine on land alſo, with ſome timber, therewith to mend our boate, that it might ſerue vs in time of næde.

The 6.of September, it was indifferent faire ſea-wether & ſunſhine, the wind being Weſt, whereby we were ſomewhat comforted, hoping that the Ice would driue away, and that we might get from thence againe.

The

The 7. of September it was indifferent wether againe, but we perceiued no opening of the water, but to the contrary it lay hard inclofed with Ice, & no water at all about the ſhip, no not ſo much as a bucket full The ſame day 5 of our men went on land, but 2 of them came backe againe, the other thrée went forward about 2 miles into the land & there found a riuer of Swéet water, where alſo they found great ſtore of wood, that had bin driuen thither, and there they foud the fote-ſteps of harts and hinds, as they thought, for they were clouen footed, ſome greater footed then others, which made them Iudge them to be ſo.

The 8. of September, it blew hard Eaſt North-eaſt, which was a right contrary wind to doe vs any good touching the carrying away of the Ice, ſo that we were ſtil faſter in the Ice, which put vs in no ſmall diſcomfort.

The 9. of September, it blew North-eaſt, with a little ſnowe, whereby our ſhip was wholy incloſed with Ice for y wind draue the Ice hard againſt it, ſo that we lay 3. or 4. foote déepe in the Ice, and our Sheck in the after ſteuer, brake in péeces, and the ſhip began to be ſomewhat looſe before, but yet it was not much hurt.

In the night time two beares came cloſe to our ſhip ſide, but we ſounded our trumpet, and ſhot at them, but hit them not, becauſe it was darke, and they ran away.

The 10. of September, the wether was ſomwhat better, becauſe the wind blew not ſo hard, and yet all one wind.

The 11. of September it was calme wether, & 8. of vs went on land, euery man armed, to ſée if that were true as our other thrée companions had ſaid, that there lay wood about the riuer, for that ſéeing we had ſo long wound and turned about, ſometime in the Ice & then againe got out, & thereby were compelled to alter our courſe, and at laſt ſawe that we could not get out of the Ice, but rather became faſter, and cou'd not looſe our ſhip, as at other times we had done, as alſo that it began to be winter, we tooke counſell together what we were beſt to doe, accoording to the time, that we might winter there, and attend ſuch aduenture, as God would ſend vs: and after we had debated vpon the matter (to kéepe and defend our ſelues both from the cold and the wild beaſts) we determined to build a houſe vpon the land, to kéepe vs therein as well

as

as we could, and so to commit our selues vnto the tuition of God, and to that end we went further into the land, to find out the conuenientest place in our opinions, to raise our house vpon, and yet we had not much stuffe to make it withall, in regard that there grew no trées nor any other thing in that country conuenient to buide it withall: but we leauing no occasion vnsought, as our men went abroad to view the country, and to sée what good fortune might happen vnto vs, at last we found an vnexpected comfort in our néed, which was, that we found certaine trées roots and all, (as our thrée companions had said before) which had bin driuen vpon the shoare, either from Tartaria, Muscouia, or else where; for there was none growing vpon that land, wherewith (as if God had purposely sent them vnto vs) we were much comforted, being in good hope, that God would shew vs some further fauour; for that wood serued vs not onely to build our house, but also to burne, and serue vs all the winter long, otherwise without all doubt, we had died there miserably with extreame cold.

How God in our extremest néed, when we were forced to lye all the winter vpon the land sent vs wod to make vs a house, and to serue vs to burne in the cold winter.

The 12 of September it was calme wether, and then our men went vnto the other side of the land, to sée if they could finde any wood néerer vnto vs, but there was none.

The 13 of September, it was calme but very misty wether, so that we could doe nothing, because it was dangerous for vs to go into the land, in regard that we could not sée the wild beares, and yet they could smell vs, for they smell better then they sée.

The 14 of September it was cléere sunshine wether, but very cold, and then we went into the land, and laid the wood in heapes one vpon the other, that it might not be couered ouer with ye snow, and from thence ment to carry it to the place where we intended to builde our house.

The 15 of September, in the morning, as one of our men held watche, wée saw thrée beares, whereof the one lay still behind a péece of Ice, the other two came close to the ship; which we perceiuing, made our péeces ready to shoote at them, at which time there stood a tub full of béefe, vpon the Ice, which lay in the water to be seasoned, for that close by the ship there was no water : one of the Beares went vnto it, and put in his head to take out a péece of the béefe, but she fared therewith, as the dog did with ye pudding, for as she was snatching at the béefe, she was shot into

the

the head wherewith she fell downe dead, and neuer stir'd: the other beare stood still, and lokt vpon her fellow, and when she had stood a good while she smelt her fellow, and perceiuing that she was dead, she ran away, but we toke halberts and other armes with vs and followed her, and at last she came againe towards vs, and we prepared our selues to withstand her, wherewith she rose vp vpon her hinder feet, thinking to rampe at vs but while she reared her selfe vp, one of our men shot her into the belly, and with that she fell vpon her fore-feet againe, and roaring as loud as she could, ran away. Then we toke the dead beare, and ript her belly open; and taking out her guts, we set her vpon her fore feet, that so she might freese as she stood, intending to carry her w vs into Holland, if we might get our ship lose, & when we had set ye beare vpon her foure feet, we began to make a slead, thereon to drawe the wood to the place where we went to build our house, at that time it froze two fingers thicke in the salt water, and it was exceeding cold, the wind blowing North-east.

The 16. of September, the sunne shone, but towards the euening it was misty, the wind being easterly, at which time we went to fetch wood with our sleads, & then we drew foure beames aboue a mile vpon the Ice and the snow, that night againe it frose aboue two fingers thicke.

The 17. of September thirtene of vs went where the wood lay, with our sleads, and so drew fiue and fiue in a slead, and the other three helped to lift the wood behind, to make vs draw the better, and with more ease and in that manner we drew wood twice a day, and laid it on a heape by the place where we ment to build our house.

The 18. of September the wind blew west, but it snowed hard, and we went on land againe to continue our labour, to draw wood to our place appointed, and after dinner the sun shone and it was calme wether.

The 19. of September, it was calme sunshine wether, and we drew two sleads full of wood fire thousand paces long, and that we did twice a day.

The 21 of September, it was misty wether, but towards euening it cleared vp, and the Ice still draue in the sea, but not so strongly as it did before, but yet it was very cold.

The

The 22 of September, it was faire still weather, but very cold, the wind being west.

The 23 of september, we fetcht more wood to build our house, which we did twice a day, but it grew to be misty and still weather againe, the wind blowing East, and East-north-East, that day our Carpenter being of purmecaet dyed, as we came aboord about euening.

The 24 of September, we buryed him, vnder the seiges, in the clift of a hill, hard by the water, for we could not dig vp the earth, by reason of the great frost and cold, and that day we went twice with our sleads to fetch wood.

The 25 of September, it was darke weather, the wind blowing West and West-south-west, and south-west, and the Ice began somewhat to open, and driue away; but it continued not long, for that hauing driuen about the length of the shot of a great Peece, it lay three fadoms deepe vpon the ground: and where we lay, the Ice draue not, for we lay in the middle of the Ice, but if we had layne in the maine sea, we would haue hoysed sayle, although it was the late in the yeare. The same day we raised vp the principles of our house, and began to worke hard thereon, but if the ship had bin loose we would haue left our building, and haue made our after Steuen of our ship, that we might haue bin ready to saile away, if it had bin possible, for that it grieued vs much to lye there all that cold winter, which we knew would fall out to be extreame bitter, but being bereaued of all hope, we were compelled to make necessity a vertue, and with patience to attend what issue God would send vs.

The 26 of September, we had a west wind and an open sea, but our ship lay fast, wherewith we were not a little grieued, but it was Gods will, which we most patiently bare, and we began to make vp our house, part of our men fetcht wood to burne, the rest played the Carpenters: and were busie about the house, as then we were sixteene men in all, for our Carpenter was dead, and of our sixteene men there was still one or other sicke.

The 27 of September it blew hard north-east, and it frose so hard, that as we put a nayle into our mouthes, (as when men worke Carpenters worke they vse to doe) there would Ice hang thereon when wee tooke it out againe, and make the blood follow,

low: the same day there came an old Beare and a yong one towards vs, as we were going to our house, being altogether (for
we durst not go alone) which we thought to shot at, but she ran a-
way, at which time the Ice came forcibly driuing in, and it was
faire sunshine weather but so extreame cold, that we could hardly
worke, but extremity forced vs thereunto.

The 28 of September, it was faire weather, and the sun shon,
the wind being west and very calme, the sea as then being open,
but our ship lay fast in the Ice and stirred not, the same day there
came a beare to the ship, but when she espied vs, she ran away and
we made as much hast as we could to build our house.

The 29. of September in the morning, the wind was West,
and afternoone it blew Northly, and then we saw three Beares
betwéene vs and the house, an old one and two yong; but we notwithstanding drew our goods from the ship to the house, and so got
before the Beares yet they followed vs: neuerthelesse we would
not shun the way for them, but hollowed out as loud as we could,
thinking that they would haue gone away, but they would not
once go out of their fote-path, but got before vs, wherewith we,
and they that were at the house, made a great noise, which made
the Beares runne away, and wée were not a little glad thereof.

The 30. of September the winde was East, East-south-east,
and all that night and the next day it snowed so fast, that our men
could fetch no wood it lay so close and high one vpon the other: then
we made a great fire without the house, therewith to thaw the
ground, that so we might lay it about the house, that it might be
the closer; but it was all lost labour, for the earth was so hard, and
frozen so déep into the ground, that we could not thaw it, and it
would haue cost vs to much wood, and therefore we were forced
to leaue off that labour.

The first of October the winde blew stiffe, North-east, after
noone it blew North, with a great storme, mist of snow, whereby we could hardly go in the winde, and a man could hardly draw
his breath, the snow draue so hard in our faces, at which time wée
could not see two ships length from vs.

The 2. of October before noone, the sun shone, and afternoone
it was cloudy againe, and it snew, but the weather was still, the

winde

winde being North, and then south, and we set vp our house, and vpon it we placed a May-pole made of frozen snowe.

The 3. of October before noone, it was calme Son-shine-weather, but so cold, that it was hard to be indured, and after noone it blew hard out of the West, with so great and extreame cold, that if it had continued, we should haue béene forced to leaue our worke.

The fourth of October, the winde was West, and after noone North, with great store of snow, whereby we could not worke: at that time we brought our Ankor vpon the Ice to lye the faster, when we lay but an arrow shot from the water, the Ice was so much driuen away.

The 5. of October, it blew hard North-west, and the Sea was very open and without Ice, as farre as we could discerne, but we lay still frozen as we did before, and our ship lay two or thrée foote déepe in the Ice, and we could not perceiue otherwise, but that we lay fast vpon the ground, and then it was thrée fadome and a halfe déepe. The same day we brake vp the lower deck of the fore-part of our ship, and with those deales we couered our houses, and made it slope ouer head, that the water might run off, at which time it was very cold.

The 6. of October it blew hard West South-west, but towards euening, West North-west, with a great snow, that we could hardly thrust our heads out of the dore, by reason of ye great cold.

The 7. of October it was indifferent good wether, but yet very cold, and we calk't our house, and brake the ground about it at the foote thereof: that day the winde went round about the compasse.

The 8. of October, all the night before, it blew so hard, and the same day also, and snowed so fast, that we should haue smothered, if we had gone out into the aire, and to speake truth, it had not béene possible for any man to haue gone one ships length, though his life had laine thereon: for it was not possible for vs to goe out of the house or ship.

The 9. of October the winde still continued North, and blew and snowed hard, all that day the wind as then blowing from the land, so that all that day we were forced to stay in the shipthe weather

ther was fo foule.

The 10. of October the weather was fomewhat fairer, and the winde calmer, and blew South-weft, and Weft, and South-weft, and that time the water flowed two foote higher then ordinary, which wee geff to proceede from the firft North wind, which as then had blowne. The fame day the wether began to bée fomewhat better, fo that we began to go out of our fhip againe: and as one of our men went out, he chaunced to méete a Beare, and bbas almoff at him before he knew it, but prefently he ranne backe againe towards the fhip, and the Beare after him; but the Beare comming to the place where before that we killed another Beare, and fet her bpright, and there let her fréeze, which after was couered ouer with Ice, and yet one of her pawes reached aboue it, fhee ftod ftill, whereby our man got before her, and clome bp into the fhip, in great feare, crying, A beare, a beare, which we hearing? came aboue hatches to looke on her, & to fhote at her, but we could not fée her, by meanes of the excéeding great fmoake, that had fo fore tormented (bs while we lay bnder hatches) in the foule wether, which we would not haue indured for any money, but by reafon of the cold and fnowy wether, we were conftrained to do it, if we would faue our liues, for aloft in the fhip we muft bndoubtedly haue dyed? the beare ftaied not long there, but run away, the wind then being North-eaft.

The fame day about euening, it was faire wether, and we went out of our fhip to the houfe, and carryed the greateft part of our bread thither.

The 11. of October it was calme wether, the wind being fouth, and fomewhat warme, and then we carryed our wine and other victuals on land: & as we were hoyfing the wine ouer-bord, there came a beare towards our fhip, that had laine behinde a péece of Ice, and it féemed that we had waked her with the noife we made: for we had féene her lye there, but we thought her to be a péece of Ice; but as fhe came néere bs, we fhot at her, and fhee ran away, fo we procéeded in our worke.

The 12. of October it blew North, and fomewhat wefterly, and then halfe of our men kept in the houfe, and that was the firft time that we lay in it, but we indured great cold, becaufe our cabins were not made; & befides that we had not clothes inough, &

we

we could kéepe no fire because our chimney was not made, whereby it smoaked exceedingly.

The 13. of October the winde was North and North-west, &
it began againe to blow hard, and then thrée of vs went a bœrd the
ship, and laded a sleade with bére, but when we had laden it, thinking to go to our house with it, sodainly there rose such a wind, &
so great a storme and cold, that we were forced to go into the ship
againe, because we were not able to stay without, and we could
not get the bére into the ship againe, but were forced to let it stand
without vpon the sleade : being in the ship, we indured extreame
cold, because we had but a few clothes in it.

The 14. of October, as we came out of the ship, we found the
barrell of bére standing vpon the sleade, but it was fast frozen at
the heads, yet by reason of the great cold, the bére that purged
out, froze as hard vpon the side of the barrel as if it had bin glewed
thereon, and in that sort we drew it to our house, and set the barrell an end, and dranke it first vp, but we were forced to melt the
bére, for there was scant any vnfrozen bére in the barrell, but in
that thicke yeast that was vnfrozen lay the strength of the bére, so
that it was to strong to drinke alone, and that which was frozen
tasted like water, and being melted we mixt one with the other,
and so dranke it, but it had neither strength nor tast.

The 15 of October the wind blew North and east, & East South
east, that day we had place to set vp our dore, and shouled the
snowe away.

The 16 of October, the wind blew South east and by South-
east, with faire calme weather : the same night there had bin a
Beare in our ship, but in the morning she went out againe, when
she saw our men : at the same time we brake vp another peece of
our ship, to vse the deales about the portall, which as then we began to make.

The 17 of October, the wind was South and South-east,
calme weather, but very cold, and that day we were busied about
our portaile.

The 18 of October, the wind blew hard East South-east, and
then we fetched our bread out of the Scute which we had drawne
vp vpon the land, and the wine also which as then was not much
frozen, and yet it had layne sire wéeks therein, and not withstand-
ding

ding that it had often times frozen very hard. The same day we saw an other beare, and then the sea was so couered ouer with Ice that we could sée no open water.

The 19 of October ý wind blew North-east, & then there was but two men & a boy in the ship, at which time there came a Beare that sought forcibly to get into the ship, although the two men shot at her with péeces of wood, and yet she ventured vpon them, whereby they were in an extreame feare, each of them séeking to saue them selues, the two men leapt into the balust, and the boy clomed into the fore mast top, to saue their liues, meane time some of our men, shot at her with a musket, and then shée ran away.

The 20 of October it was calme sunshine weather, and then againe we saw the sea open, at which time we went on bord to fetch the rest of our béere out of the ship, where we found some of the barrels frozen in péeces, and the Iron heapes that were vpon the Iosam barrels were also frozen in péeces.

The 21 of October, it was calme sunshine wether, and then we had almost fetched all our victuals out of the ship.

The 22 of October, the wind blew coldly, and very stiff North-east, with so great a snow, that we could not get out of our dores.

The 23 of October, it was calme weather, and the wind blew North-east, then we went abord our ship, to sée if the rest of our men would come home to the house; but wée feared ý it would blow hard againe, and therefore durst not stirre with the sicke man, but let him ly still that day, for he was very weake.

The 24. of October, the rest of our men being 8. persons, came to the house, and drew the sicke man vpon a slead, and then with great labour and paine, we drew our boate home to our house, and turned the bottome thereof vpwards, that when time serued vs (if God saued our liues in the Winter time) wée might vse it: and after that, perceiuing that the ship lay fast, and that there was nothing lesse to be expected then the opening of the water, we put our Anchor into the ship againe, because it should not be couered ouer and lost in the snow, that in the spring time wée might vse it: for wée alwaies trusted in GOD that hée

would

would deliuer vs from thence towards Sommer time, either one way or other.

Things ſtanding at this point with vs, as the ſunne, when wée might ſée it beſt and higheſt, began to be very low, we vſed all the ſpéede we could to fetch all things with ſleades out of our ſhip into our houſe, not onely meate and drinke, but all other neceſſaries, at which time the winde was North.

The 25. of October, we fetcht all things that were neceſſary for the furniſhing of our Scute and our Boate: and when we had laden the laſt ſlead, and ſtood ready to draw it to the houſe, our maiſter loked about him and ſaw thrée Beares behind the ſhip that were comming towards vs, whereupon he cryed out aloud to feare them away, & we preſently leaped forth to defend our ſelues as well as we could: and, as good fortune was, there lay two halberds vpon the ſlead, whereof the maſter toke one, and I the other, and made reſiſtance againſt them, as well as we could; but the reſt of our men ran to ſaue themſelues in the ſhip, and as they ran, one of them fell into a clift of Ice, which gréeued vs much: for we thought verily that the beares would haue ran vnto him, to deuoure him, but God defended him: for the Beares ſtill made towards the ſhip after the men ẏ ran thither to ſaue themſelues. Meane time, we and the man that fel into the clift of Ice, toke our aduantage, and got into the ſhip on the other ſide, which the Beares perceiuing, they came fiercely towards vs, that had no other armes to defend vs withall, but onely the two halberds, which wee doubting would not be ſufficient, wee ſtill gaue them worke to do by throwing billets and other things at them, and euery time we threw, they ran after them as a dogge vſeth to doe at a ſtone that is caſt at him. Meane time we ſent a man down vnder hatches to ſtrike fire, and another to fetch pikes, but wee could get no fire, and ſo we had no meanes to ſhote: at the laſt as the Beares came fiercely vpon vs, we ſtroke one of them with a halberd vpon the ſnoute, wherewith ſhe gaue back, when ſhee felt her ſelfe hurt, and went away, which the other two ẏ were not ſo great as ſhe, perceiuing, ran away: and we thanked God that wee were ſo well deliuered from them, & ſo drew our ſlead quietly to our houſe, and there ſhewed our men what had happened vnto vs.

The

The 26. of October the wind was North, and North-North-West, with indifferent faire wether: then we saw open water hard by the land, but we perceiued the Ice to driue in the sea, still towards the ship.

The 27. of October, the wind blew North-east, and it snowed so fast, that we could not worke without the dore That day our men kil'd a white For, which they flead: and after they had rosted it, ate thereof, which tasted like Connies flesh: the same day we set vp our diall, and made the clock strike, and we hung vp a lamp to burne in the night time, wherein we vsed the fat of the beare, which we molt and burnt in the lampe.

The 28. of October, wee had the wind North-east, and then our men went out to fetch wood, but there fell so stormy wether, and so great a snow, that they were forced to come home againe: about euening the wether began to breake vp, at which time three of our men wen to the place where we had set the beare vpright, and there stood frozen, thinking to pull out her teeth, but it was cleane couered ouer with snow: and while they were there, it began to snow so fast againe, that they were glad to come home, as fast as they could; but the snow beat so sore vpon them, that they could hardly see their way, & had almost lost their right way, whereby they had like to haue laine all that night out of the house.

The 29. of October the wind still blew North-east, & then we fetch'd segges from the Sea side, & laid them vpon the saile, that was spread vpon our house, that it might be so much the closer & warmer: for the deales were not driuen close together, and the foule wether would not permit vs to do it.

The 30. of October, the wind yet continued North-east, and then the Sunne was full aboue the earth, a little aboue the Horison.

The 31. of October, the wind still blew North-east, wt great store of snow, whereby we durst not looke out of dores.

The first of Nouember the wind still continued North-east, & then we saw the moone rise in the East when it began to be darke, and the Sunne was no higher aboue the Horizon than wee could well see it, and yet that day we saw it not, because of the close we-ther and the great snow that fell, and it was extreame cold, so that

L   we we could not go out of the house.

The 2. of Nouember, the Wind blew West, and somewhat South, but in the euening it blew North, with calme wether, and that day we saw the Sunne rise South, South-east, and it went downe South South West, but it was not full aboue the earth, but passed in the Horizon along by the earth : and the same day one of our men killed a For with a hatchet, which was flead, rosted and eaten: before the Sunne began to decline, wee saw no Fores, and then the Beares vsed to go from vs.

The 3. of Nouember the Wind blew North-West wᵗ calme wether, and the Sunne rose South and by East, and somewhat more southerly, and went downe South and by West, and somewhat more Southerly; and then we could see nothing but the vpper part of the Sun aboue the Horizon, and yet the land where we were, was as high as the mast of our ship, then we toke the height of the Sunne, it being in the eleuenth degrée, and 48. minutes off Scorpio, his declination being 15. degrées and 24. minutes on the South side of the Equinoctiall line.

The 4. of Nouember it was calme wether, but then we saw the Sunne no more, for it was no longer aboue the Horizon, then our Chirurgion made a bath (to bathe vs in) of a Wine pipe, wherein we entred one after the other, and it did vs much good, and was a great meanes of our health. The same day wee toke a white For, that often times came abroad, not as they vsed at other times : for that when the Beares left vs at the setting of the Sunne, and came not againe before it rose, the For to the contrary came abroad when they were gone.

The 5. of Nouember the wind was North, & somewhat West, and then we saw open water vpon the Sea, but our ship lay still fast in the Ice, and when the Sunne had left vs, we saw ye Moone continually both day and night, and neuer went downe when it as in the highest degrée.

The 6. of Nouember, the wind was North-West, still wether, and then our men fetcht a slead full of fire-wood, but by reason that the Son was not séene, it was very dark wether.

The 7. of Nouember it was darke wether, and very still, the wind West, at which time we could hardly discerne the day from the night, specially because at that time our clock stood still,

and

and by that meanes we knew not when it was day, although it was day, and our men rose not out of their Cabens all that day; but onely to make water, and therefore they knew not whether the light they saw, was the light of the day or of the Moone, whereupō they were of seueral opinions, some saying it was the light of the day, the others of the night: but as we tooke good regard thereunto, we found it to be the light of the day, about twelue of the clock at noone.

The 8. of Nouember, it was still wether, the wind blowing South, and South-West. The same day our men fetcht another stead of firewood, and then also we tooke a white Fox, and saw open water in the Sea. The same day we shared our bread amōgst vs, each man hauing foure pound and ten ounces, for his allowance in eight daies, so that then we were eight daies eating a barrell of bread, whereas before we ate it vp in fiue or sixe daies: we had no néed to share our flesh and fish, for we had more store thereof, but our drinke failed vs, and therefore we were forced to share that also: but our best béere was for the most part wholly without any strength, so that it had no sauour at all: and besides all this, there was a great deale of it spilt.

The 9. of Nouember the wind blew North-east, and somewhat more Northerly, and then we had not much day-light, but it was altogether darke.

The 10 of Nouember, it was calme wether, the wind North-West, and then our men went into the ship to sée how it lay, and wée saw that there was a great deale of water in it, so that the balast was couered ouer with water, but that it was frozen, and so might not be pump't out.

The 11. of Nouember it was indifferent wether, the wind North-west: the same day we made a round thing of cable yearn, like to a net, to catch Foxes withall, that we might get them into the house, & it was made like a trap, which fell vpon the Foxes as they came vnder it, and that day we caught one.

The 12. of Nouember the wind blew East, with a little light: that day we began to share our wine, euery man had two glasses a day, but commonly our drinke was water, which we molt out of snow which we gathered without the house.

The 13. of Nouember it was foule wether, with great snow,

L 2   the

the wind East.

The 14. of Nouember it was faire cleare wether, with a cleare sky, full of starres, and an East-wind.

The 15. of Nouember it was darke wether, the wind North-east, with a vading light.

The 16. of Nouember it was wether with a temperate aire, and an East-wind.

The 17. of Nouember it was darke wether, and a close aire, the wind East.

The 18. of Nouember it was foule wether, the wind South-east: then the maiſter cut vp a packe of courſe clothes, and diuided it amongſt our men that nǽded it, therewith to defend vs better from the cold.

The 19. of Nouember, it was foule weather, with an East wind, and then the cheſt with linnin was opened, and deuided a-mongſt the men for ſhift, for they had nǽd of them, for then our onely care was to find all the means we could to defend our body from the cold.

The 20. of Nouember, it was faire ſtil weather, the wind East-erly, then we waſht our ſhǽts, but it was ſo cold, that when we had waſht and wrong them, they preſently froze ſo ſtiffe, that al-though we lay'd them by a great fire, the ſide that lay next the fire thawed, but the other ſide was hard frozen, ſo that we ſhould ſo-ner haue torne them in ſunder then haue opened them, whereby we were forced to put them into the ſǽthing water againe to thaw them, it wasſo excǽding cold.

The 21. of Nouember, it was indifferent wether with a North-east-wind, then wee agrǽd that euery man ſhould take his turne to cleaue wood, thereby to eaſe our cooke, that had more then worke inough to doe twice a day to dreſſe meat, & to melt ſnowe for our drinke, but our Maſter & the Pilot, were exempted from ȳ work.

The 22. of Nouember, the wind was ſouth-eſt, it was faire we-ther, then we had but ſeuentǽne chǽſes, whereof one we ate a-monſt vs, and the reſt were deuided to euery man one, for his portion, which they might eate when he liſt.

The 23. of Nouember, it was indifferent good weather, the wind South east, and as we perceiued that the For vſed to come oftner, and more then they were woont, to take them the better,

we

we made certaine traps of thicke plancks, wheron we laid stones, & round about them placed péeces of Shards fast in the ground, that they might not dig vnder them, and so got some of the foxes.

The 24. of Nouember, it was foule weather, & the winde North-east, & then we prepared our selues to go into the bath, for some of vs were not very well at ease, and so foure of vs went into it, and when we came out, our Surgion gaue vs a purgation, which did vs much good, and that day we tooke foure Foxes.

The 25. of Nouember, it was faire cleare weather, the winde West; and that day we tooke two foxes, with a springs that we had purposely set vp.

The 26. of Nouember, it was foule weather, and a great storme with a South-west wind, and great store of snowe, whereby we were so closed vp in the house, that we could not goe out, but were forced to ease our selues within the house.

The 27. of Nouember, it was faire cleare weather, the wind South-west, and then we made moxe Springes to get Fors, for it stood vs vpon to doe it, because they serued vs for meat, as if God had sent them purposely for vs, for wée had not much meate.

The 28. of Nouember, it was foule stormie weather, and the wind blew hard out of the North, and it snew hard, whereby we were shut vp againe in our house, the snow lay so closed before the doxes.

The 29. of Nouember, it was faire cleare wether, & a good aire: the wind Northerly, and we found meanes to open our doxe, by shoueling away the snowe, whereby we got one of our doxes open, and going out, we found al our Traps and Springes cleane couered ouer with snow, which we made cleane, and set them vp again to take Foxes: and that day we tooke one, which as then serued vs not onely for meat, but of the skins we made Caps to were vpon our heads, therewith to kéepe them warme from the extreame cold.

The 30. of Nouember, it was faire cleare weather, the wind West, and fire of vs went to the ship, all wel prouided of arms to sée how it lay: and when we went vnder the fore decke, we tooke a Fore aliue in the ship.

The 1. of December, it was foule weather with a South-west

wind

wind, and great sloare of snow, whereby we were once againe stopt vp in the house, & by that meanes there was so great a smoke in the house, that we could hardly make fire, and so were forced to lye all day in our cabens; but the Cooke was forced to make fire to dresse our meat.

The 2. of December, it was still foule weather, whereby we were forced to keep stil in the house, & yet we could hardly sit by the fire, because of the smoake, and therefore stayd still in our cabens, and then we heated stones, which we put into our Cabens to warm our feet, for that both the cold and the smoke were vnsuppor-table.

The 3. of December we had the like weather, at which time as we lay in our Cabans, we might heare the Ice crack in the sea, and yet it was at the least halfe a mile from vs, whichmade a hugh noyse, and we were of oppinion, that as then the great hils of Ice which we had seene in the sea, in summer time, brake one from the other, & for that during those 2. or 3. dayes, because of the extream smoake, we made not so much fire as we commonly vsed to doe, it froze so sore within the house, that the wals and the roofe thereof were frozen two fingers thick with Ice, and also in our Cabans where we lay all those three daies, while we could not goe out: by reason of the foule weather, we set vp the glas of 12. houres, & whe it was run out, we set it vp againe, stil watching it lest we should misse our time. For the cold was so great, that our Clock was fro-zen, and might not goe, although we hung more waight on it then before.

The 4. of December, it was faire cleare weather, the wind Northeast, and then we began euery man by turne to dig open our dores that were closed vp with snow, for we saw that it would be often to doe, and therefore we agreed to work by turns, no man excepted but the Maister and the Pilot.

The 5. of December, it was faire weather, with an East-wind and then we made our Springes cleane againe to take Foxes.

The 6 of December, it was foule weather againe, with an Easterly wind, and extreame cold, almost not to be indured, wher-upon we lookt pittifully one vpon the other; being in great feare, that if the extremity of the cold grew to be more & more, we should all die there with cold, for that what fire soeuer we made, it would

not

not warme vs, yea and our fack which is fo hotte, was frozen very hard, fo that when we were euery man to haue his part, we were forced to melt it in the fire, which we fhared euery fecond day about halfe a pint for a man, wherewith we were forced to fuftain our felues, and at other times we dranck water, which agreed not well with the cold, and we needed not to coole it with fnowe or Ice, but we were forced to melt it out of the fnow.

The 7. of December, it was ftill foule weather, and we had a great ftorme, with a North-eaft-wind, which brought an extreame cold with it, at which time we knew not what to do, & while we fate confulting together, what were beft for vs to do, one of our companions gaue vs counfell to burne fome of the fea-coles that we had brought out of the fhip, which would caft a great heat and continue long, and fo at euening we made a great fire thereof, which caft a great heat : at which time we were very carefull to keepe it in : for that the heat being fo great a comfort vnto vs, we tooke care how to make it continue long : whereupon wee agreed to ftop vp all the dores and the chimney, thereby to keepe in the heate, and fo went into our cabans to fleepe, well comforted with the heat, and fo lay a great while talking together; but at laft we were taken with a great fwounding and dafeling in our heads, yet fome more then other fome, which we firft perceiued by a fick man, and therefore the leffe able to beare it, & found our felues to be very ill at eafe, fo that fome of vs that were ftrongeft, ftart out of their cabans, and firft opened the chimney, and then the dores, but he that opened the dore fell downe in a fwound vppon the fnow, which I hearing, as lying in my Caban next to the dore, ftart vp, and cafting vinegar in his face, recouered him againe, and fo he rofe vp : and when the dores were open, we all recouered our healthes againe, by reafon of the cold aire. and fo the cold which before had beene fo great an enemy vnto vs, was then the onely reliefe that we had, otherwife without doubt, we had died in a fodaine fwound, after y̆ the Mafter, when we were come to our felues againe, gaue euery one of vs a little wine to comfort our hearts.

The 8. of December, it was foule weather, the wind Northerly, very fharpe and cold, but we durft lay no more coles on, as we did the day before, for that our misfortune had taught vs, that to

shun

shun one danger we should not run into an other.

The 9. of December, it was faire cleare weather, the skie full of Starres, then we set our dooze wide open, which befoze was fast closed vp with snowe, and made our Spzinges ready to take Foxes.

The 10. of December it was still faire Star-light weather, the wind Noxth-east: then we toke two Foxes, which were good meate fox vs, fox as then our victuals began to be scant, and the cold still increased, whereunto their skins serued vs fox a good defence.

The 11. of December, it was faire weather, and a cleare aire, but very cold, which he that felt not would not beléeue, fox our shoos froze as hard as hoznes vpon our féet, and within, they were white frozen, so that we could not weare our shwes, but were forced to make great pattens, ẏ vpper part being ship skins, which we put one ouer thzée oz foure paire of socks, and so went in them to kéepe our féet warms.

The 12. of December, it was faire cleare weather, with a Noxth-west-wind, but extreame cold, so that our house walles and Cabans where frozen a finger thicke, yea and the clothes vpon our backs were white ouer with frost, and although some of vs were of opinion that we should lay moze coles vpon the fire to warme vs, and that we should let the chimney stand open, yet we durst not do it, fearing the like danger we had escaped.

The 13. of December it was faire cleare wether, with an East wind: then we toke another For, and toke great paines about pzeparing and dzessing of our spzinges, with no small trouble, fox that if we staied too long without the doozes, there arose blisters vpon our faces and our eares.

The 14. of December it was faire wether, the wind Noxth-east, and the sky full of starres, then we toke the height of ẏ right shoulber of the Rens. When it was South South-west, (somewhat moze Westerly (and then it was, at the highest in our compas) and it was eleuated aboue the Hozison twenty degrées and twenty eight minutes, his declination being six degrées, and eightéene minutson the Noxth side of the lyne, which declination being taken out of the height afozesaid there rested fourtéen degrées, which being také out of 90. degrées, then the height of ẏ pole was seuenty

six,

fire degrees.

The 15 of December it was still faire weather, the wind East, that day we toke two Foxes: and saw the Moone rise East-south-east, when it was twenty-fire daies old, in the signe of Scorpio.

The 16. of December, it was faire cleare weather, the wind East: at that time we had no more wood in the house, but had burnt it all, but round about our house there lay some couered ouer with snow, which with great paine and labour we were forced to digge out and so shouell away the snow, and so brought it into the house, which we did by turns, two and two together, wherin we were forced to vse great speede, for we could not long endure without the house, because of the extreame cold, although we ware the Foxes skinnes about our heads, and double apparell vpon our backs.

The 17. of December, the wind still held North east, with faire weather and so great frosts, that we were of opinion, that if there stood a barrell full of water without the doore, it would in one night freeze from the top to the bottome.

The 18. of December, the wind still held North-east, with faire wether: then seuen of vs went out vnto the ship, to see how it lay, and being vnder the decke, thinking to find a Fox there, we sought all the holes, but we found none; but when we entred into the Caben, and had stricken fire to see in what case the ship was, and whether the water rose higher in it, there wee found a Fox, which we toke, and carried it home, and eate it, and then we found that in eighteene dayes absence (for it was so long since we had beene there) the water was risen about a finger high, but yet it was all Ice, for it froze as fast as it came in, and the vessels which we had brought with vs full of fresh water out of Holland, were frozen to the ground.

The 19. of December it was faire wether, the wind being South, then we put each other in good comfort, that the sun was then almost halfe ouer, and ready to come to vs againe, which we sore longed for, it being a weary time for vs to be without the Sunne, and to want the greatest comfort that God sendeth vnto man here vpon the earth, and that w reioiceth euery liuing thing.

The 20. Dece. before noone, it was faire cleare wether, and then

M we

we had taken a Fox, but towards euening there rose such a storm in the South-west, with so great a snow that all the house was incosed therewith.

The 21. of December it was faire cleere wether, with a North-east wind, then we made our doore cleane againe, and made away to go out, and clensed our traps for the Fores, which did vs great pleasure when we tooke them, for they seemed as dainty as Uenison vnto vs

The 22. of December it was foule wether with great store of snow, the wind South-west, which stopt vp our doore againe, and we were forced to dig it open againe, which was almost euery day to do.

The 23. of December it was foule wether, the wind South-west, with great store of snow, but we were in good comfort that the Sunne would come againe to vs, for as we gest, that day he was in Tropicus Capricorni, which is the furthest signe that the sunne passeth on the South side of the line, and from thence it turneth North-ward againe. This Tropicus Capricorni lyeth on the South side of the Equinoctiall line, in twenty three degrees and eightéene minutes.

The 24. of December being Christmas Euen, it was faire wether, then we opened doore againe, and saw much open water in the sea: for we had heard the Ice crack and driue although it was not day, yet we could sée so farre: towards euening it blew hard out of the North-east, with great store of snow, so that all the passage that wee had made open before, was stopt vp againe.

The 25. of December being Christmas day, it was foule wether with a North-west wind, and yet though it was foule wether, we hard the Fores run ouer our house, wherewith some of our men said it was an ill signe, and while we sate disputing why it should be an ill signe, some of our men made answere, that it was an ill signe because we could not take them, to put them into the pot to rost them, for that had béene a very good signe for vs.

The 26. of December it was foule wether, the wind North-west, and it was so cold that we could not warme vs, although we vsed all the meanes we could, with great fires, good store of clothes, and with hot stones, and billets laid vpon our féete and
vpon

vpon our bodies, as we lay in our Cabens, but notwithstanding all this, in the morning our Cabens were frozen, which made vs behold one the other with sad countenance, but yet we comforted our selues againe as well as we could, that the Sunne was then as low as it could goe, and that it now began to come to vs againe, and we found it to be true: for that the daies beginning to lengthen, the cold began to strengthen, but hope put vs in good comfort, and eased our paine.

The 27. of December it was still foule wether, with a North-West wind, so that as then we had not bœne out in thrœ daies together, nor durst not thrust our heads out of dores, and within the house it was so extreme cold, that as we sate before a great fire, and sœmed to burne on the fore side, we froze behinde at our backs, and were al white as the country men vse to be when they come in at the gates of the towne in Holland with their sleads, and haue gone all night.

The 28. of December it was still foule wether, with a West-wind, but about euening it began to cleare vp, at which time one of our men made a hole open at one of our dores, and went out to sœ what news abroad, but found it so hard wether that he stayed not long, and told vs that it had snowed so much that the Snow lay higher then our house, and that if he had stayed out longer, his eares would vndoubtedly haue bœne frozen off.

The 29. of December it was calme wether, and a pleasant aire the wind being Southward: that day, he, whose turne it was, opened the dore, and dig'd a hole through the snow, where wee went out of the house vpon steps, as if it had bin out of a Seller, at least seuen or eight steps high, each step a fote from the other, and then we made cleane our springes for the Foxes, whereof for certaine daies we had not taken any, and as we made them cleane, one of our men found a dead Fox in one of them, that was frozen as hard as a stone, which he brought into the house, and thawed it before the fire, and after fleaing it, some of our men ate it.

The 30. of December it was foule wether againe, with a storme out of the West, and great store of snow, so that all the labour and paine that we had taken the day before to make steps, to go out of our house, and to clense our springes, was al in vaine,

for

for it was al couered ouer w̄ snow againe, higher thē it was before.

The 31. of December it was still foule wether, with a storme out of the North-west, whereby we were so fast shut vp into the house, as if we had béene prisoners, and it was so extreame cold, that the fire almost cast no heate: for as we put our féete to the fire, we burnt our hose before we could féele the heate, so that we had work inough to do to patch our hose: and which is more, if we had not sooner sinel, then selt them, we should haue burnt them ere we had knowne it.

After that with great cold, danger, & disease, we had brought this yeare vnto an end, we entred into ȳ yeare of our Lord God 1597. ȳ beginning whereof, was in ȳ same maner as ȳ end of Anno 1596. had béene for the wether continued as cold, foule, snowy as it was before, so that vpon the first of Ianuary we were inclosed in the house ȳ wind thē being West, at the same time we agréed to share our wine euery man a small measure full, and that but once in two daies: and as we were in great care and feare that it would be long before we should get out frō thence, (& we hauing but sinal hope therin) some of vs spared to drink wine as long as wée could, that if we should stay long there, we might drinke it at our néede.

The 2. of Ianuary, it blew hard, with a West wind, and a great storme, with both snow and frost, so that in four or fiue daies we durst not put our heads out of ȳ dores, & as then by reason of the great cold, we had almost burnt all our wood, notwithstanding we durst not goe out to fetch more wood, because it froze so hard, & there was no being without the dore, but séeking about we found some péeces of wood, that lay ouer the dore, which we cloue, and withall cloue the blocks whereon we vsed to beate our stock-fish, and so holp our selues so well as we could.

The 3. of Ianuary, it was all one weather, and we had little wood to burne.

The 4. of Ianuary, it was still foule stormie weather, with much snow and great cold, the wind South-west, and we were forced to kéepe in the house: and to know where the wind blew, we thrust a halfe pike out at ȳ chimney, w̄a little cloth, or fether vpon it, but as soone as we thrust it out, it was presently frozen, as hard as a péece of wood, and could not go about nor stirre with the wind.

The 5. of Ianuary, it was somewhat still and calme weather, then

then we digd our dore open againe, that we might goe out, and carry out all the filth, that had bin made during the time of o ur being ſhut in the houſe; and made euery thing handſome, and fetched in wood, which we cleft, and it was all our dayes worke to further our ſelues as much as we could, fearing leſt we ſhould be ſhut vp againe: and as there were three dores in our portall, and for y̓ our houſe lay couered ouer in ſnow, we tooke y̓ middle dore thereof away, and digged a great hole in the ſnow, that laie with out the houſe, like to a ſide of a vault, wherein we might go to eaſe ourſelues, and caſt other filth into it: and when we had taken paines al day, we remembred our ſelues that it was Twelf Euen, & then we prayed our Maiſter that we might be merry that night, and ſaid that we were content to ſpend ſome of the wine that night, which we had ſpared, and which was our ſhare euery ſe cond day, and whereof for certaine daies we had not drunke; and ſo that night we made merry, and drunke to the three Kings, and therewith we had two pound of meale, whereof we made pan cakes with oyle, and euery man a white biſket, which we ſopt in wine: and ſo ſuppoſing that we were in our owne country, and a mongſt our frends, it comforted vs as well as if we had made a great banket in our owne houſe: and we alſo made tickets, and our Gunner was king of Noua Zembla, which is at leaſt two hun dred miles long, and lyeth betweene two ſeas.

The 6 of Ianuary, it was faire weather, the wind north eaſt, then we went out and clenſed our Traps to take Foxes. which were our Ueniſon, a nd we digd a great hole in the ſnow, where our fire wood lay, and left it cloſe aboue like a vault; & from thence fetcht out our wood as we needed it.

The 7. of Ianuary, it was foule weather againe, with a North weſt wind, and ſome ſnow, and very cold, which put vs in great feare, to be ſhut vp in the houſe againe.

The 8. of Ianuary, it was faire weather againe, the wind North. then we made our Springes ready to get more Ue neſon: which we longed for, and then we might ſee and marke dya light, which then began to increaſe, that the Sunne as then began to come towards vs againe, which put vs in no litle comfort.

The 9. of Ianuary, it was foule wether, with a North wcſt wind, but not ſo hard wether as it had bin before, ſo y̓ we might go

out

out of the dooze, to make cleane our Springes, but it was no néed to bid vs goe home againe, for the cold taught vs by experience not to stay long out, for it was not so warm to get any good by staying in the aire.

The 10. of Ianuary, it was faire weather, with a North-wind: they seuen of vs went to our ship, well armed, which we found in the same state we left it sin, and it we saw many fotesteps of Beares, both great and small, whereby it séemed that there had bin moze then one oz two Beares therein; and as we went vnder hatches, we strooke fire, and lighted a candle, and found that the water was rysen a fote higher in the ship.

The 11. of Ianuary, it was faire weather, the wind North-east, and the cold began to be somewhat lesse, so that as then we were bold to goe out of the doozes, and went about a quarter of a mile to a hill, from whence we fetched certaine stones, which we layd in the fire, therewith to warme vs in our Cabans.

The 12. of Ianuary, it was faire cleare weather, the wind North-west : that euening it was very cleare and the skie full of Stars, then we toke the height of Occulus Tauri, which is a bright and well knowne Star, & we found it to be eleuated aboue ý Horison twenty nine degrées and fifty foure minuts, her declination being fiftéene degrées, fifty foure minutes on the North side of the lyne . This declination being substracted from the height aforesaid, then there rested fourtéene degrées, which substracted from ninety degrées, then the height of the pole was seuenty fire degrées, and so by measuring the height of that starre, and some others we gesse that ý Sun was in the like height, and that we were there vnder seuenty fire degrées, and rather higher then lower.

The 13. of Ianuary, it was faire still weather the wind west-sterlie, and then we perceaued that day-light began moze and moze to increase, and wee went out and cast bullets at the bale of ý flag staffe, which before we could not sée when it turnd about.

The 14. of Ianuary, it was faire weather, and a cleare light, the wind Westerlie, and that day we toke a Fox.

The 15. of Ianuary, it was faire cleare weather, with a West wind, and six of vs went abozd the ship, where we found, the bolck-banger, (which the last time that we were in the ship, we stucke in a hole in the foze decke, to take Foxes) puld out of the hole, and lay

in

in the middle of the ship, and al torne in péces by the Bears as we perceiued by their foote-steps.

The 16. of January, it was faire weather, the wind Northerly, and then we went now & then out of the house to strech out our ioynts and our lūnes with going and running, that we might not become lame, and about noone time we saw certaine rednes in the skie (as a shew or missen ger of the Sunne that began to come towards vs.

The 17. of January, it was cleare weather, with a North wind, and then still more and more wée perceiued that the Sun began to come neerer vnto vs, for the day was somewhat warmer, so that when wee had a good fire, there fell great péces of Ice downe from the walles of our house, and the Ice melted in our cabens, and the water dropt downe, which was not so before, how great soeuer our fire was, but that night it was cold againe.

The 18. of January, it was faire cleare weather, with a southeast wind, then our wood began to consume, & so we agréed to burne some of our sea-coles, and not to stop vp the chimney, and then wée should not néede to feare any hurt, which wée did, and found no disease thereby, but we thought it better for vs to kéepe the coles, and to burne our wood more sparingly, for that the coles wold serue vs better when we should saile home in our open Scute.

The 19. of January, it was faire weather, with a North wind, and then our bread began to diminish, for that some of our barels were not full waight, & so the diuision was lesse, and we were forced to mak our allowance bigger with that which we had spared before: and then some of vs went abord the ship, wherein there was halfe a barrell of bread, which we thought to spare till the last, and there secretly each of them tooke a bisket or two out of it.

The 20. of January, the ayre was cleare, and the wind southwest, that day we staied in the house, and cloue wood to burne and brake some of our emptie barrels, and cast the Iron hoopes vpon the top of the house.

The 21. of January, it was faire weather, with a West wind, at that ime taking of Foxes began to faile vs, which was a siane that they Beares would soone come againe, as not long after we

found

found it to be true, for as long as the Beares ſtay away, the Foxes came abroad, and not much before the Beares come abroad, the Foxes were but little ſéene.

The 22. of January, it was faire wether with a Weſt wind, then we went out againe to caſt the bullet, and perceiued that day light began to appeare, whereby ſome of vs ſaid, that the Sun would ſone appeare vnto vs, but William Barents to the contrary ſaid, that it was yet two wéeks to ſone.

The 23. of January, it was faire calme weather, with a South-weſt-wind, then foure of vs went to the ſhip, and comforted each other, giuing God thankes, that the hardeſt time of the winter was paſt, being in good hope that we ſhould liue to talke of thoſe things at home in our owne country, and when we were in the ſhip, we found that the water roſe higher and higher in it, and ſo each of vs taking a biſket or two with vs, we went home againe.

The 24. of January, it was faire cleare weather, with a Weſt wind: then I, and Iacob Hemskecke, and another with vs went to the ſea ſide, on the South ſide of Noua Zembla, where contrary to our expectation, I firſt ſaw the edge of the Sun, where with we went ſpœdily home againe, to tell Willam Barents and the reſt of our companions that ioyfull newes: but William Barents being a wiſe and well experienced pilot would not beléeue it, eſtéemingit to be about fourtœne daies to ſone, for the Sunne to ſhin in that part of the world, but we earneſtly affirmed the contrary, and ſaid that we had ſéene the Sunne.

The 25. & 26. of January it was miſty, and cloſe weather, ſo ẏ we could not ſée any thing, then they that layd ẏ contrary wager wt vs, thought that they had won, but vpon the twenty ſeuen day it was cleare weather, and then we ſaw the Sunne in his full roundneſſe aboue the Horiſon, whereby it manfeſtly appeared that we had ſéene it vpon the twenty foure day of January. And as we were of diuers opinions touching the ſame, and that we

How the Sun which they had loſt, the 4. of Nouember did appere to them again vpon the ſaid it was cleane contrary to the opinions of all olde and newe wꝛiters, yea and contrary to the nature and roundneſſe both of Heauen and Earth; ſome of vs ſaid, that ſéeing in long tims there had béen no day, that it might be that we had ouerſlept our ſelues, whereof we were better aſſured : but concerning the thing in it ſelfe,

selfe, seeing God is wonderfull in all his workes, we will referre that to his almightie power, and leaue it vnto others to dispute of, but for that no man shall thinke vs to be in doubt thereof, if we should let this passe without discoursing vpon it, therefore we will make some declaration thereof, whereby we may assure our selues that we kept good reckening.

24. of Ianuary which was very strange, and contrary to all learned mens opinions.

You must vnderstand, that when we first saw the Sunne, it was in the fift degree and 25. minutes of Aquarius, and it should haue staied according to our first gessing, till it had entred into the sirtéenth degree and 27. minutes of Aquarius, before he should haue shewed there vnto vs, in the higth of 76. degrées.

Which we striuing and contending about it, amongst our selues, we could not be satisfied, but wondred thereat, and amongst vs were of opinion, that we had mistaken our selues, which neuerthelesse, we could be perswaded vnto, for that euery day, without faile we noted what had past, and also had vsed our clocke continually, and when that was frosen, we vsed our houre-glasse of 12. houres long, whereupon we argued with our selues, in diuers wise, to know how we should finde out that difference, and leaue the truth of the time, which to trie we agrée to looke into the Ephemerides made by Iosephus Schala, printed in Venice, for the yéeres of our Lord 1589. till a 1600. and we found therein, that vpon the 24. day of Ianuary, (when the Sunne first appeared vnto vs) that at Venice the clocke being one in the night time, the Moone and Iupiter were in coniunction, whereupon we sought to knowe when the same coniunction should be ouer or about the house where we then were, and at last we found, ў the 24. day of Ianuary was the same day, whereon the coniunctiō aforesaid happened in Venice, at one of the clocke in the night, & with vs in the morning, when ў Sun was in the east: for we saw manifestly, that the two Planets afore said, approached néere vnto each other, vntill such time as the Moone & Iupiter stood one iust ouer the other, both in the signe of Taurus, and that was at sir of the clocke in the morning, at which time the Moone and Iupiter were found by our Compas to be in coniunction, ouer our house, in the North and by east point, & the South part of the Compas was south-south-west, and there we had it right south, the Moone being eight daies old, whereby it appeareth, that the

Sunne

Sunne and the Moone were eight points different, and this was about sixe of the clocke in the morning: this place differeth from Venice fiue houres in longitude, whereby we maye gesse how much we were nearer east then the Citie of Venice, which was fiue houres, each houre being 15. degrees, which is in all 75. degrees, that we were more easterly then Venice, by all which it is manifestly to be seene, that we had not failed in our account, and that also we had found our right longitude, by the two Planets aforesaid, for the towne of Venice lieth vnder 37. degrees and 25. minutes in longitude, and her declination is 46. degrees and 5. minutes, whereby it followeth that our place of Noua Zembla, lieth vnder 112. degrees and 25. minutes in longitude, and the higth of the Pole 76. degrees, and so you haue the right longitude & latitude, but frō the vttermost point of Noua Zembla, to ye point of Cape de Tabin, the vttermost point of Tartaria, where it windeth southward: The longitude differeth 60. degrees, but you must vnderstand, that the degrees are not so great, as they are vnder the Equinoxial line, for right vnder the line a degree is fifteene miles, but when you leaue the line, either northward or southward, then the degrees in longitude do lessen, so that the nearer that a man is to the North or South Pole, so much the degrees are lesse: so that vnder the 76. degrees northward, where wee wintered, the degrees are but 3. miles, and ⅓ parts, whereby it is to be marked, that we had but 60. degrees to saile to the said Cape de Tabin, which is 220. miles, so the said Cape lieth in 172. degrees in longitude as it is thought: and being aboue it, it seemeth that we should be in the straight of Anian, where we may saile bouldlie into the South, as the land reacheth: Now what further instructions are to be had to know where we lost the sun vnder ye said 76. degrees vpon the fourth of Nouember, & saw it againe vpon the 24. of Ianuary: I leaue that to be described, by such as make profession thereof, it suffiseth vs to haue shewed, that it failed vs not to appeare at the ordinary time.

The 25. of Ianuary, it was darke clowdy weather, the wind Westerlie, so that the seeing of the Sunne the day before, was againe doubted of, and then many wagers were laid, and we still lookt out to see if the Sunne appeared, the same day we sawe a Beare, (which as long as the Sunne appeared not vnto vs we sawe said not) comming out of the south west towards our house, but when we shouted at her she came no nærer, but went away againe.

The 26. of Ianurie, it was faire clære weather, but in the Horrison there hung a white or darke clowde, whereby we could not sée the Sun, whereupon the rest of our companions, thought that we had mistaken our selues vpon the 24. day, and that the Sunne appeared not vnto vs, and mocked vs, but we were resolute in our former affirmation, that we had sæne the Sunne, but not in the full round nesse: That euening the sicke man that was amongst vs, was very weake, and felt him selfe to be extreame sicke, for he had laine long time, and we comforted him as well as we might, & gaue him the best admonition ẏ we could, but he died not long after midnight.

The 27. of Ianuarie it was faire clære weather, with a southwest winde, then in the morning we digd a hole in the snowe, hard by the house, but it was still so extreame cold, that we could not stay long at worke, and so we digd by turnes, euery man a litle while, and then went to the fire, and an other went and supplyed his place, till at last we digd seauen foote depth, wherewe went to burie the dead man, after that when we had read certaine chapters and sung some Psalmes, we all went out and buried the man, which done we went in and brake our fasts, and while we were at meate, and discoursed amongst our selues, touching the great quantitie of snowe that continually fell in that place, wee said that if it fell out, that our house should be closed vp againe with snowe, we would find the meanes to climbe out at the chimney whereupon our master went to trie if he could climbe vp through the chimney, and so get out, and while he was climbing one of our men went forth of the dore, to sée if the master were out or not, who standing vpon the snowe, saw the Sunne, and called vs all out, wherewith we all went forth and saw the Sunne in his full roundnesse, a litle aboue the horrison, and then it was without all doubt, that we had sæne the Sunne vpon the 24. of Ianuarie, which made vs all glad, and we gaue God hearty thankes, for his grace shewed vnto vs, that that glorious light appeared vnto vs againe.

The 28. of Ianuary, it was faire weather, with a west wind,

then

then we went out many tymes to exercife our felues, by going, running, cafting of the ball, (for then we might fee a good way from vs) and to refrefh our ioynts, for we had long time fitten dull, whereby many of vs were very loafe.

The 29 of Ianuary, it was foule weather with great ftore of fnow, the wind North-weft, whereby the houfe was clofed vp againe with fnow.

The 30. of Ianuary, it was darke weather, with an Eaft-wind, and we made a hole through the doore, but we ſhoueled not the, fnow very farre from the portaile, for that as foone as we faw what weather it was, we had no defire to goe abroad.

The 31. of Ianuary, it was faire calme weather, with an Eaft-wind, then we made the doore cleane, and ſhoueled away the fnow, and threw it vpon the houfe, and went out, and we faw not the Sun ſhine cleare, which comforted vs, meane time we faw a Beare, that came towards our houfe, but we went foftly in, and watcht for her till ſhe came neerer, and as foone ſhe was hard by we ſhot at her, but ſhe ran away againe.

The 1. of February, being Candlemas eue, it was boifterous weather, with a great ftorme and good ftore of fnow, whereby the houfe was clofed vp againe with fnow, and we were couftrained to ftay within doores, the wind then being North-weft,

The 2. of February, it was foule weather, and as then the Sun had not rid vs of all the foule weather, whereby we were fome what difcomforted, for that being in good hope of better weather we had not made fo great prouifion of wood as wee did before.

The 3. of February, it was faire weather, with an Eaftwinde, but very mifty, whereby we could not fee the Sun, which made vs fomewhat melancholy, to fee fo great a miffe, and rather more then we had had in the winter time, and then we digd our doore, open againe, and fetcht the wood that lay without about the doore into the houfe, which we were forced with great paine and labour to dig out of the fnow.

The 4. of February, it was foule weather, with great ftore of fnow, the wind being South-weft, and then we were clofe vpagaine with fnow, but then we toke not fo much paines as we did before, to dig open the doore, but when we had occafion or goe out we

we climed out at the chimney, and eaſed our ſelues, and went in a-
gaine the ſame way.

The 5. of February it was ſtill foule weather, the wind being
Eaſt, with great ſtore of ſnow, whereby we were ſhut vp againe
into the houſe, and had no other way to get out but by the chimney,
and thoſe that could not climbe out were faine to helpe themſelues,
within as well as they could.

The 6. of February it was ſtill foule ſtormie weather, with ſtore
of ſnow, and we ſtill went out at the chimney, (and troubled not
our ſelues with the doore,) for ſome of vs made it an eaſie matter
to climbe out at the chimney.

The 7. of February, it was ſtil foule weather, with much ſnow
and a South-weſt wind, and we thereby forced to keepe the houſe,
which grieued vs more then when the Sun ſhined not, for that hauing ſeen it and felt the heat thereof, yet we were forced not to in-
ioy it.

The 8. of February, it began to be fairer weather, the wind being South-weſt, thē we ſaw the Sun riſe South South-eaſt, and
went downe South, South-weſt, by ẏ compas that wehad made
of lead, and placed accordingto the right meridian of that place,
but by our common co mpas, it differed. two pointe.

The 9. of February, it was faire cleare weather, the wind
South-weſt, but as then we could not ſee the Sunne, becauſe it
was cloſe weather in the South, where the Sunne ſhould goe
downe.

The 10, of February, it was faire cleare weather, ſo that we
could not tell where the wind blew, and thē we began to feele ſome
heat of the Sunne, but in the euening it began to blow ſomewhat
cold out of the weſt.

The 11.of February, it was faire weather, the wind South, ẏ
day about noone, there came a Beare towards our houſe, and we
watcht her with our Muskets, but ſhe came not ſo neere that wee
could reach her, the ſame night we heard ſome Foxes ſtirring,
which ſince the beares began to come abroad againe, we had much
ſeen.

The 12. of February, it was cleare weather and very calme,
the wind South-weſt, then we made our traps cleane againe,
meane time there came a great Beare towards our houſe, which

N 3   made

made vs all goe,in and we leauelled at her with our muskets,and
as she came right befoze our doze,we shot her into the bzeast,clean
thzough the heart, the bullet passing thzough her body and went
ont againe at her tayle, and was as flat as a counter. the Beare
feeling the blow, lept backwards and ran twenty oz thirty fote
from the house, and there lay downe, wherewith we lept all out of
the house and ran to her,and found her stil aliue,and when she saw
vs,she reard vp her head,as if she would gladly haue done vs some
mischefe,but we trusted her not,foz that wehad tryed their stregth
sufficiently befoze,and therefoze we shot their twice into the body
againe, and therewith she dyed, then we ript vp her belly, and taking out her guts dzew her home to the house,where we slead her,
and toke at least one hundzed pound of fat out of her belly, which
we molt, and burnt in our Lampe. This grease did vs great god
seruice,foz by that meanes we stil kept a Lampe burning all night
long which befoze we could not doe,foz want of grease,and euery
man had meanes to burne a Lamp in his Cabyn, foz such necessaries as he had to doe.The Beares skin was nine fote long, and 7
fote bzoad.

The 13 of Febzuary, it was faire cleare weather with a hard
West wind,at which time we had moze light in our house by burning of Lamps,whereby we had meanes to passe the time away,by
reading and other exercises, which befoze (when we could not dis-
tinguish day from night, by reason of the darknesse, and had not
Lamps continually burning) we could not doe.

The 14. of Febzuary, it was faire clere weather, with a hard
west wind befoze none, but after none, it was still weather, then
fiue of vs went to the ship , to see how it laie, and found the water to encrease in it, but not much.

The 15. of Febzuary, it was foule weather, with a great
stozme out of the south-west , with great stoze of snowe , whereby the house was closed vp againe , that night the Foxes came to
deuoure the dead body of the Beare , whereby we were in great
feare., that all the Beares thereabouts would come theither,and
therefoze we agreed , as sone as we could to get out of the house
to bury the dead Beare deepe vnder the snowe.

The 16. of Febzuary, it was still foule weather with great
stoze of snowe,t a south-west wind, that day was Shzoue-twes-

day

day, then wee made our selues some what merry in our great griefe and trouble, and euery one of vs dranke a draught of wine in remembrance that winter began to weare away, and faire weather to approach.

The 17. of February, it was still foule weather and a darke sky, the wind South, then we opened our doze againe, and swept away the snow. and then we thrue the dead Beare into the hoale where we had digd out some wood, and stoypt it vp, that the Beares by smelling it, should not come thither to trouble vs, and we set vp our springes againe to take Foxes, and the same day fiue of vs went to the ship, to sée how it laie, which we found all after one sort, there we found foote-steps of many Beares, as though they had taken it vp for their lodging, when we had forsaken it.

The 18. of February, it was foule weather with much snow and very cold, the wind being south-west, and in the night time as we burnt lampes, and some of our men laie awake, we heard beasts runne vpon the roofe of our house, which by reason of the snowe, made the noise of their féete sound moze, then otherwise it would haue done, the snow was so hard, whereby we thought they had béene Beares, but when it was day, we sawe no footing but of Foxes, and we thought they had béene Beares, for the night which of it selfe is solitarie and fearefull, made that which was doubtfull to be moze doubtfull and worse feared.

The 19. of February, it was faire cleere weather, with a southwest wind, then we tooke the hight of the Sunne, which in long time before we could not doe, because the Horizon was not cleere, as also for that it mounted not so high, nor gaue not so much shadowe, as we were to haue in our Astrolabium, and therefore we made an instrument, that was halfe round, at the one end hauing 90. degrées marked thereon, whereon we hung a thrid with a Plumet of lead, as the water compasses haue, and therewith we tooke the hight of the Sunne, when it was at the highest, and found that it was thrée degrées eleuated aboue the Horizon, his declination eleuenth degrées and sirtéene minutes, which béeing added to the hight aforesaid, made 14. degrées ɬ 16. minutes, which substracted from 90. degrées, there rested 75. degrées and 44. minutes for the higth of the Pole, but the aforesaid thrée degrées of higth, being taken at the lowest side of the Sunne, the

16.

16. minutes might well be added to the higth of the Pole, and so it was iust 76. degrées, as we had measured it before.

The 20. of Febzuary, it was foule weather with great stoze of snow, the wind south-west, whereby we were shut vp againe in the house, as we had béene often times before.

The 21. of Febzuary, it was still foule weather, the wind nozth-west, and great stoze of snow, which made vs greiue moze then it did before, foz we had no moze wood, & so were forced to bzeake of some péeces of wood in the house, and to gather vp some that lay troden vnder féet, which had not bin cast out of the way, whereby foz that day and the next night we holp our selues indifferent well.

The 22 of Febzuary it was clere faire weather, with a South-west wind, then we made ready a slead to fetch moze wood, foz néed compelled vs thereunto, foz as they say hunger dziueth the Wolfe out of his den, and eleuen of vs went together, all well appointed with our armes, but coming to the place where wee should haue the wood, we could not come by it, by reason it laie so déepe vnder the snow, whereby of necessitie we were compelled to goe further, where with great labour and trouble we got some: but as we returned backe againe therewith, it was so soze labour vnto vs that we wers almost out of comfozt, foz that by reason of the long cold and trouble that we had indured, we were become so weake & féeble, that we had litle strength, & we began to be indoubt, that we should not recouer our strengths againe, and should not be able to fetch any moze wood, and so we should haue died with cold, but the pzesent necessitie, and the hope we had of better weather, increased our fozces, and made vs doe moze then our strengthes affozded, and when we came néere to our house, we saw much open water in the Sea, which in long time we had not séene, which also put vs in good comfozt, that things would be better.

The 23. of Febzuary, it was calme and faire weather, with a good aire, the wind south-west, and then we tooke two Foxes, that were as good to vs as venison.

The 25. of Febzuary, it was still weather, and a close aire, the wind south-west, then we dzest our spzinges in good sozt, foz the Foxes, but tooke none.

The 25, of Febzuary, it was foule weather againe, and much snow,

with a Noʒth wind, whereby we were clofed vp with ſnowa-
gaine, and could not get out of our houſe.

The 26. of Febʒuary, it was darke weather, with a ſouth-
weſt wind, but very calme, and then we opened our dooʒe againe,
and exerciſed our ſelues with going and running, and to make
our ioints ſupple, which were almoſt clinged together.

The 27. of Febʒuary, it was calme weather, with a South
wind, but very cold, then our wood began to leſſen, which put vs
in no ſmall diſcomfoʒt, to remember what trouble we had to dʒaw
the laſt ſlead-full home, and we muſt doe the like againe, if we
would not die with cold.

The 28. of Febʒuary, it was ſtill weather with a ſouth-weſt
wind, then ten of vs went and fetcht and other ſlead-full of wood,
with no leſſe paine and laboʒ then we did befoʒe, foʒ one of our
companions could not helpe vs, becauſe that the firſt ioint of one
of his great toes was froʒen of, and ſo he could doe nothing.

The firſt of March, it was faire ſtill weather, the wind weſt,
but very cold, and we were foʒced to ſpare our wood, becauſe it
was ſo great laboʒ foʒ vs to fetch it, ſo that when it was day, we
exerciſed our ſelues as much as we might, with running, going,
and leaping, and to them that laie in their Cabins, we gaue
hote ſtones to warme them, and towards night we made a good
fire, which we were foʒced to indure.

The 2. of Marche, it was cold cleare weather, with a Weſt
wind, the ſame day we tooke the higth of the Sunne, and found
that it was eleuated aboue the Hoʒizon ſixe degrées and 48. minutes, and his declination was 7 degrées and 12. minutes, which
ſubſtracted from 90. degrées, reſteth 76. degrees foʒ the higth of
the Pole.

The 3. of March, it was faire weather with a Weſt wind, at
which time our ſickemen were ſomewhat better, and ſat vpright
in their Cabins, to doe ſome thing to paſſe the time awaie, but after they found that they were too ready to ſtirre befoʒe their times.

The 4. of March, it was faire weather with a Weſt wind,
the ſame day there came a Beare to our houſe, whom we watcht
wᵗ our péeces, as we did befoʒe, & ſhot at her & hit her, but ſhe run
away, at that time fiue of vs went to our ſhip, where we found
that the Beares had made woʒke, & had opened our Cookes cub-

D

bert

berd, that was couered ouer with ſnow, thinking to finde ſome thing in it, and had drawne it out of the ſhip where we found it.

The 5. of March, it was foule weather againe, with a ſouth-weſt wind, and as in the euening we had digd open our doꝛe and went out, when the weather began to bꝛeake vp, we ſaw much open water in the Sea, moꝛe then befoꝛe, which put vs in good comfoꝛt, that in the end we ſhould get away from thence.

The 6. of March, it was foule weather, with a great ſtoꝛme out of the ſouth-weſt, and much ſnow, the ſame day ſome of vs climbed out of the chimney and perceaued that in the Sea, and a-bout the land there was much open water, but the ſhip lay faſt ſtill.

The 7. of March, it was ſtill foule weather and as great a wind, ſo that we were ſhut vp in our houſe, and they that would goe out, muſt clime vp thꝛough the chimney, which was a common thing with vs, and ſtill we ſawe moꝛe open water in the Sea, and about the land, whereby we were in doubt that the ſhip in that foule weather and dꝛiuing of the Ice, would be looſe (foꝛ as then the Ice dꝛaue) while we were ſhut vp in our houſe, and we ſhould haue no meanes to helpe it.

The 8. of Marche, it was ſtill foule weather, with a ſouth-weſt ſtoꝛme, and great ſtoꝛe of ſnow, whereby we could ſée no Ice in the noꝛth-eaſt, noꝛ round about in the Sea, wereby we were of opinion that noꝛth-eaſt from vs, there was a great Sea.

The 9. of March it was foule weather, but not ſo foule as the day befoꝛe, and leſſe ſnow, and then we could ſée further from vs, and perceiue that the water was open in the noꝛth-eaſt, but not from vs towards Tartaria, foꝛ there we could ſtill ſée Ice in the Tartarian Sea, otherwiſe called the Ice Sea, ſo that we were of opinion, that there it was not very wide, foꝛ when it was cléere weather, we thought many times that we ſaw the land, and ſhowed it vnto our companions, ſouth and ſouth-eaſt from our houſe, like a hilly land, as land commonly ſhoweth it ſelfe, when we ſée it.

The 10. of March, it was cléere weather, the wind Noꝛth, then we made our houſe cleane, and digd our ſelues out, and came foꝛth, at which time we ſaw an open Sea, whereupon we ſaid vnto each other, that if the ſhip were looſe, we might venture to

ſaile

saile aſwaie, foz we were not of opinion to doe it with our Scutes, conſidering the great cold that we found there: towards euening, nine of vs went to the ſhip with a ſlead to fetch wood, when al our wood was burnt, and found the ſhip in the ſame ozder that it laie an d faſt in the Ice.

The 11. of March, it was cold, but faire ſunne-ſhing weather, the wind nozth-eaſt, then we twke the higth of the Sunne, with our Aſtrolabium, and found it to be eleuated aboue the Hozizon ten degrées and 19. minutes, his declination was thzée degrées 41. minutes, which being added to the higth afozeſaid, made 14. degrées, which ſubſtracted from 90. degrées, there reſteth 76. degrées foz the higth of the Pole: then twelue of vs went to the place where we vſed to goe, to fetch a ſlead of wood, but ſtill we. had moze paine and labour therewith, becauſe we were wea- ker, and when we came home with it and were very weary we pzaid the maſter to giue either of vs a dzaught of wine, which he did, wherewith we were ſomewhat reléeued, & comfozted, and after that were the willinger to labour, which was vnſuppozta- ble foz vs, if méere extremitie had not compelled vs thereunto, ſaying often times one vnto the other, that if the wood were to be bought foz mony, we would giue all our earnings, oz wages foz it.

The 12 of. March, it was foule weather, ẙ wind nozth-eaſt, then the Ice came mightily dziuing in, which the south-weſt winde had bin dziuen out, and it was then as could, as it had bin befoze in the coldeſt time of winter.

The 13. of March, it was ſtill foule weather, with a ſtozme out of the Nozth-eaſt, and great ſtoze of ſnow, and the Ice mightely dziuing in with a great noyſe, the flakes ruſtling againſt each o- ther fearfull to heare.

The 14. of March, it was ſtill foule weather with a great eaſt Nozth-eaſt wind, wherby the ſea was as cloſe as it had bin befoze, and it was extreame cold, whereby our ſicke men were very ill, who when it was faire weather, were ſtirring too ſoone.

The 15. of march, it was faire weather, the wind Nozth, that day we opened our doze to goe out, but the cold rather increaſed then diminiſhed, and was bitterer then befoze it had bin.

The 16 of March, it was faire cleare weather, but extreame cold with a Nozth wind, which put vs to great extremity, foz that

we

we had almost taken our leaues of the cold, and then it began to come againe.

The 17 of March it was faire cleare weather, with a North-wind, but stil very cold, wherby wée were wholy out of comfort, to sée and féele so great cold, and knew not what to thinke, for it was extreame cold.

The 18. of March, it was foule cold weather, with good store of snow the wind North-east, which shut vs vp in our house, so that we could not get out.

The 19. of March, it was still foule and bitter cold weather, the wind North-east, the Ice in the sea cleauing faster and thicker together, with great cracking, and a hugh noyse, which we might easily heare in our house, but we delighted not much in hearing thereof.

The 20. of March, it was foule weather, bitter cold, and a North-east wind, then our wood began to consume, so that we were forced to take counsell together, for without wood we could not liue, and yet we began to be so weake, that we could hardly endure the labour to fetch it.

The 21. of March, it was faire weather, but still very cold, the wind North the same day the Sunne entred into Aries, in the equinoctiall lyne, and at noone we tooke the hight of the Sunne, and found it to be eleuated 14.degrées aboue the Horizon, but for that the Sun was in the middle lyne, and of the like distance from both the tropiks, there was no declination, neither on the South nor north side, and so the 14. degrées aforesaid being substracted, from ninty degrées, there rested 76 degrées for the hight of the Pole. The same day, we made shoes of felt or rudg, which we drew vpon our féet, for we could not goe in our shoes, by reason of the great cold, for the shoes on our féet were as hard as hornes, and then we fetcht a stead-ful of wood home to our house, with sore and extreame labour, and with great extremity of cold which we endured, as if March went to bid vs farewell, for our hope and comfort was that the cold could not still continue in that force, but that at length the strength thereof would be broken.

The 22. of March, it was cléere still weather, the wind North-east, but very cold, whereupon some of vs were of aduice, séeing that the fetching of wood was so toylsome vnto vs, that euery day once

once we should make a fire of coales.

The 23. of March, it was very foule weather, with infernall bitter cold, the wind North-east, so that we were forced to make more fire, as we had bin at other times, for then it was as cold as euer it had bin, and it froze very hard in the flore and vpon the wales of our house.

The 24. of March, it was alike cold, with great store of snow, and a North wind, whereby we were once againe shut vp into the house, and then the coalls serued vs well, which before by reason of our bad vsing of them, we disliked of.

The 25. of March, it was still foule weather, the wind west, the cold still holding as strong as it was: which put vs in much discomfort.

The 26. of March, it was faire cleere weather, and very calme, then we digd our selues out of the house againe, and went out, & then we fetcht an other slead of wood, for the great cold had made vs burne vp all that we had.

The 27. of March, it was faire weather, the wind west and very calme, then the Ice began to driue away againe, but the ship lay fast and stird not.

The 18. of March, it was faire weather, the wind South-west, whereby the Ice draue away very fast. The same day sixe of vs went aboord the ship, to see how it lay, and found it still in one sort; but we perceiued that the Beares had kept an euil fauoured house therein.

The 29. of March, it was faire cleere weather, with a North-east wind, then the Ice came driuing in againe, the same day we fecht another slead of wood, which we were euery day worse alike to doe, by reason of our weaknesse.

The 30. of March, it was faire cleere weather, with an East wind, wherwith the Ice came driuing in againe; after noone there came two Bears by our house, but they went along to the ship, and let vs alone.

The 31. of March, it was still faire weather, the wind North-east, where with the Ice came still more and more driuing in, and made high hilles by sliding one vpon the other.

The 1. of Aprill, it blew stil out of the East, with faire weather

D 3

but

but very cold, and then we burnt some of our coales, for that our
wood was too troublesome for vs to fetch.

The 2. of Aprill , it was faire weather , the wind north-
east and very calme, then we tooke the higth of the Sunne and
found it to be eleuated aboue the Horizon 18. degrées and 40. minutes, his declination being foure degrées and 40. minutes,
which being subftracted from the higth aforesaid , there refted 14.
degrées , which taken from 90. degrées, the higth of the Pole was
76. degrées.

The 3. of Aprill it was faire cléere weather, with a north-eaft
wind, and very calme, then we made a ftaffe to plaie at colfe, thereby to ftretch our Jointes , which we fought by all the meanes we
could to doe.

The 4. of Aprill, it was faire weather , the wind variable,
that daie we went all to the ſhip and put out the cable that was
made faſt to the anchor, to the end that if the ſhip chanced to be
loofe, it might hold faſt thereby.

The 5. of Aprill it was foule weather, with a hard north-eaft
wind , wherewith the Ice came mightily in againe , and flid in
great péeces one vpon the other, and then the ſhip laie faſter then
it did before.

The 6. of Aprill , it was ſtill foule weather , with a ſtiffe north-
weſt wind , that night there came a Beare to our houſe , and we
did the beſt we could to ſhoot at her , but becauſe it was moiſt
weather, & the cocke foiſtie , our péece would not giue fire, wherewith the Beare came bouldly toward the houſe , and came downe
the ſtaires close to the dore , ſéeking to breake in to the houſe but
our maſter held the dore faſt to , & being in great haſte and feare,
could not barre it with the péce of wood that we vſed thereunto,
but the Beare ſéeing that the dore was ſhut, ſhe went backe a-
gaine, and within two houres after ſhe came againe, and went
round about and vpon the top of the houſe, and made ſuch a roaring , that it was fearefull to heare, and at laſt got to the chimney,
and made ſuch worke there , that we thought ſhe would haue
broken it downe, and tore the ſaile that was made faſt about it
in many péeces , with a great and fearefull noiſe, but for that it
was night we made no reſiſtance againſt her , becauſe we could
not ſée her , at laſt ſhe went awaie and left vs.

The

The 7. of Apꝛill, it was foule weather, the wind south-west, then we made our muskets ready, thinking the Beare would haue come againe, but she came not, then we went vp vpon the house, where we saw what foꝛce the Beare had vsed, to teare away the saile, which was made so fast vnto the chimney.

The 8. of Apꝛill, it was still foule weather, the wind south-west, whereby the Ice dꝛaue away againe, and the Sea was open, which put vs in some comfoꝛt, that we should once get away out of that fearefull place.

The 9. of Apꝛill, it was faire cléere weather, but towards euening it was foule weather, the wind South-west, so that stil ŷ water became opener, whereat we much reioysed, and gaue God thanks that he had saued vs from the afoꝛesaid cold, troublesome, hard, bitter, and vnsuppoꝛtable Winter, hoping that time would giue vs a happy issue.

The 10. of Apꝛill it was foule weather, with a stoꝛme out of the Noꝛth-east, with great stoꝛe of snowe at which time the Ice, that dꝛaue away, came in againe, and couered all the sea ouer.

The 11. of Apꝛill, it was faire weather, with a great Noꝛth-east wind, wherewith the Ice still dꝛaue one péece vpon another, and lay in high hilles.

The 21. of Apꝛill, it was faire cléere weather, but still it blew hard Noꝛth-east, as it had done two dayes befoꝛe, so that the Ice lay like hilles one vpon the other, and then was higher and harder then it had bin befoꝛe.

The 13. of Apꝛill, it was faire cléere weather, with a Noꝛth wind, the same day we fetcht a stead with wood, & euery man put on his shwoes, that he had made of felt oꝛ rudg, which did vs great pleasure.

The 14. of Apꝛill, it was faire cleare weather, with a West wind, then we saw greater hilles of Ice round about the ship, then euer we had séene befoꝛe, which was a fearefull thing to behold, and much to be wondꝛed at, that the ship was not smitten in péeces.

The 15. of Apꝛill, it was faire calme weather with a Noꝛth wind, then seauen of vs went aboard the ship, to sée in what case it was, and found it to be all in one soꝛt, and as we came backe againe, there came a great Beare towards vs, against whom we
began

began to make defence, but she perceauing that, made away from vs, and we went to the place from whence she came, to sée her den, where we found a great hole made in ye Ice, about a más lenght in depth, the entry thereof being very narrow, and with in, wide, there we thrust in our pickes to féele if there was any thing within it, but perceauing it was emptie, one of our men crept into it, but not too farre, fo2 it was fearefull to behold, after that we went along by the Sea side, and there we saw, that in the end of March, and the begining of Ap2ill the Ice was in such wondefull maner risen and piled vp one vpon the other, that it was wonderfull in such manner as if there had bin whole townes made of Ice, with tow2es and bulwarkes round about them.

The 16. of Ap2ill it was foule weather, the wind no2th-west, whereby the Ice began some-what to b2eake.

The 17. of Ap2ill it was faire cléere weather, with a south-west wind, and then seauen of vs went to the ship, and there we saw open water in the Sea , and then we went ouer the Ice-hilles as well as we could to the water, fo2 in sir o2 seauen monthes we had not gone so neare vnto it, and when we got to ye water, there we saw a litle bird swiming therein, but as soone as it espied vs, it diued vnder the water, which we tooke fo2 a signe that there was mo2e open water in the Sea, then there had béene befo2e, and that the time app2oached that the water would open.

The 18. of Ap2ill, it was faire weather, the wind south-west, then we tooke the higth of the Sunne, and it was eleuated aboue the Ho2lzon 25. degrées and 10. minutes, his declination 11. degrées and 12. minutes, which being taken from the higth afo2e-said, there rested 13. degrées and 58. minutes, which subst2acted from 90. degrées, the higth of the Pole was found to be 75. degrées, 58. minutes; then eleuen of vs went with a slead to fetch mo2e wood, and b2ought it to the house: in the night there came as other Beare vpon our house, which we hearing, went all out with our armes, but the Beare ranne away.

The 19. of Ap2ill it was faire weather with a No2th wind, that day fiue of vs went into the bath, to bathe our selues, which did vs much good, and was a great refreshing vnto vs.

The 20. of Ap2ill, it was faire weather with a West wind, the same day fiue of vs went to the place where we fetcht wood,

with

with a kettle & other furniture vpon a sead, to wash our shirts in that place, because the wood lay ready there, and for that we were to vse much wood to melt the Ice, to heate our water, and to drie our shirtes, esteming it a lesse labour, then to bring the wood home to the house which was great trouble vnto vs.

The 21. of Aprill it was faire weather, with an East wind, and the next day the like weather, but in the euening the wind blewe northerly.

The 23. of Aprill, it was faire weather, and a north-east wind, and the next day the like, with an East wind,

The 25. of Aprill, it was faire weather, the wind easterly, the same day there came a Beare to our house, and we shoot her into the skin, but she runne awaie, which another Beare that was not farre from vs perceauing runne away also.

The 26. and 27. of Aprill it was faire weather, but an extreme great north-east wind.

The 28. of Aprill it was faire weather, with a North wind, then we tooke the higth of the Sunne againe, and found it to be eleuated 28. degrees and 8. minutes, his declination 14. degrees and 8. minutes, which subtracted from 90. degrees, there rested 76. degrees for the higth of the Pole.

The 29. of Aprill it was faire weather, with a south-west wind, then we plaid at colfe, both to the ship, and from thence againe homeward, to exercise our selues.

The 30. of Aprill it was faire weather, the wind south-west, then in the night we could see the Sunne in the North (when it was in the highest) iust aboue the Horizon, so that from that time we saw the Sunne both night and day.

The 1. of May, it was faire weather with a West wind, then we sod our last flesh, which for a long time we had spared, and it was still very good, and the last morsell tasted as well as the first, and we found no fault therein, but onely that it would last no longer.

The 2. of May, it was foule weather, with a storme out of the south-west, whereby the Sea was almost cleere of Ice, and then we began to speake about getting from thence, for we had kept house long enough there.

The 3. of May it was still foule weather, with a south-west
P
wind

wind, whereby the Ice began wholy to driue away, but it lay fast about the ship, and when our best meate, as flesh, and other things began to faile vs, which was our greatest sustenance, and that it behoued vs to be somewhat strong, to sustaine the labour that we were to vndergoe, when we went from thence, the master shared the rest of the Bacon amongst vs, which was a small barrell with salt Bacon in pickle, whereof euery one of vs had two ounces a day, which continued for the space of three weekes, and then it was eaten vp.

The 4 of May it was indifferent faire weather, ȳ wind south-west, that day flue of vs went to the ship, and found it lying still as fast in the Ice as it did before, for about the midle of March it was but 75 paces from the open water, and then it was 500 paces from the water, and inclosed round about with high hilles of Ice, which put vs in no small feare, how we should bring our Scute and our boate through or ouer that way into the water: when we went to leaue that place, that night there came a Beare to our house, but as soone as she heard vs make a noise, she ranne away againe, one of our men that climbed vp in the chimney saw when she ranne away, so that it seemed that as then they were afraid of vs, and durst not be so bold to set vpon vs, as they were at the first.

The 5 of May, it was faire weather, with some snow, the wind East, that euening, and at night we saw the Sunne when it was at the lowest, a good way aboue the Earth.

The 6 of May, it was faire cleare weather, with a great south-west wind, whereby we saw the Sea open both in the East and in the West, which made our men excéeding glad, longing sore to be gone from thence.

The 7 of May, it was foule weather, and snow hard, with a North wind, whereby we were closed vp againe in our house, whereupon our men were somewhat disquieted, saying that they thought they should neuer goe from thence, and therefore said they, it is best for vs as soone as it is open water to be gone from hence.

The 8 of May, it was foule weather, with great store of snow, the wind West, then some of our men agréed amongst themselues to speake vnto the master, and to tell him that it was more
then

then time for vs to be gone from thence, but they could not agree vpon it, who should moue the same vnto him, becaufe he had faid that he would ſtaie vntill the end of June, which was the beſt of the ſommer, to ſee if the ſhip would then be looſe.

The 9. of May it was faire cleere weather, w an indifferent wind out of the north-eaſt, at which time the deſire that our men had to be gone from thence, ſtill more and more encreaſed, and then they agreed to ſpeake to Willam Barents, to moue the maſter to goe from thence, but he held them of with faire words, and yet it was not done to delay them, but to take the beſt counfell, with reaſon and god aduiſe, for he heard all what they could faie.

The 10. of May, it was faire weather with a North-weſt wind, y night the Sun by our common compas being North, North-eaſt, and at the loweſt, we tooke the higth thereof, and it was eleuated 3 degrees and 45 minutes, his declination was 17 degrees and 45 minuts, from whence taking the higth aforeſaid, there reſted 14. degrees, which ſubſtracted from 90 degrees, there reſted 76 degrees for the higth of the Pole.

The 11. of May, it was faire weather, the wind South-weſt, and then it was open water, in the ſea, then our men prayed William Barents once againe to moue the Maiſter to make preparation to goe from thence, which he promiſed to do as ſoone as conue-nient time ſerued him.

The 12. of May, it was foule weather, the wind North-weſt & then the water became ſtill opener then it was, which put vs in god comfort.

The 13. of May, it was ſtill weather, but it ſnowed hard with a North wind.

The 14. of May, we fetcht our laſt ſlead with fire wod, and ſtil ware our ſhoes made of rugde on our feete, wherewith we did our ſelues much pleaſure, and they furthered vs much: at the ſame time we ſpake to Willam Barents againe, to moue the maiſter a-bout going from thence, which he promiſed he would doe.

The 15. of May, it was faire weather, with a weſt wind, and it was agreed that all our men ſhould goe out, to exerciſe their bo-dies with running, goeing, playing at colfe and other exerciſes, thereby to ſtirre their ioynts and make them nymble, meane time Barents ſpake vnto the maiſter, and ſhowed him what the com-

P 2   pany

pany had said, who made him answeare that they should stay no longer then to the end of that Mounth, & that if then the ship could not be losed, that preparation should be made to goe away with the Scute and the boate.

The 16 of May, it was faire weather, with a West-wind at which time, the company were glad of the answere that the Maister had giuen, but they thought the time too long, because they were to haue much time to make the boate and the Scute ready to put to Sea with them, and therefore some of them were of opinion that it would be best for them to sawe the boate in the middle, and to make it longer, which opinion thought it was not amisse, neuerthelesse it would be y worse for vs, for that although it should be so much the better for the sailing, it would be so much the vnfitter to be drawne ouer the Ice, which we were forced to doe.

The 17. and 18, of May, it was faire cleere weather, with a West wind, and then we began to reconne the daies that were set downe and appointed for vs to make preparation to be gone.

The 19. of May it was faire weather with an East wind, then foure of our men went to the ship, or to the sea side, to see what way we should draue the Scute into the water.

The 20. of May, it was foule weather with a North-east wind, whereby the Ice began to come in againe, and at noone we spake vnto the Maister, & told him that it was time to make preparation to be gon, if we would euer get away from thence, whereunto he made answeare, that his owne life was as deere vnto him, as any of ours vnto vs, neuerthelesse he willed vs to make haste to prepare our clothes, and other things ready and fit for our voiage, and that in the meane time we should patch and amend them, that after it might be no hinderance vnto vs, and that we should stay till the Mounth of May was past, and then make ready the Scute and the boate, and al other things fit and conuenient for our Journey.

The 21. of May, it was faire weather, with a North-east wind, so that the Ice came driuing in againe, yet we made preparation, touching our things that we should weare, that we might not be hindred thereby.

The 22. of May, it was faire weather, with a North-west wind, and

and for that we had almoſt ſpent all our wood, we brake the portall of our doze downe and burnt it.

The 23. of May, it was faire weather with an Eaſt wind, then ſome of went againe to the place where the wood lay to waſh our ſheets.

The 24. of May, it was faire weather, with a South-eaſt wind, whereby there was but a little open water.

The 25. of May, it was faire weather, with an Eaſt wind, then at noone tune we tooke the higth of the Sunne, that was eleuated aboue the Horizon 34 degrées and 46 minutes, his declination 20 degrées and 46 minutes, which taken from the higth aforeſaid, there reſted 14 degrées, which taken from 90 degrées, reſted 76 degrées, for the higth of the pole.

The 26. of May, it was faire weather, with a great North-eaſt wind, whereby the Ice came in againe.

The 27. of May, it was foule weather, with a great North-eaſt wind, which draue the Ice mightely in againe, whereupon the Maiſter, at the motion of the company willed vs to make preparation to be gon.

The 28. of May, it was foule weather, with a North-weſt wind, after noone it began to be ſomewhat better, then ſeuen of vs went vnto the ſhip, and fetcht ſuch things from thence, as ſhould ſerue vs for the furniſhing of our Scute, and our boate, as the old fock ſayle, to make a ſayle for our boate, and our Scute, and ſome tackles, and other things neceſſarie for vs.

The 29. of May, in the morning, it was reaſonable faire weather with a Weſt wind, then ten of vs went vnto the Scute to bring it to the houſe to dreſſe it, and make it ready to ſayle, but we found it déepe hidden vnder ẏ ſnow, & were faine with great paine and labour to dig it out, but when we had gotten it out of the ſnow, and thought to draw it to the houſe, we could not doe it, becauſe we were too weake, wherewith we became wholely out of heart, doubting that we ſhould not be able to goe forwarde with our labour, but the Maiſter encouraging vs, bad vs ſtriue to doe moze then we were able, ſaying that both our liues and our welfare conſiſted therein: and that if we could not get the Scute from thence, and make it ready, then he ſaid we muſt dwell there as Burgers of Noua Zembla, and make our graues in that place but

there

there wanted no good will in vs but onely strength, which made vs for that time to leaue of worke and let the Scute lye still, which was no small griefe vnto vs, and trouble to thinke what were best for vs to doe, but after none being thus comfortlesse come home, we tooke hearts againe and determined, to tourne the boate that lay by the house with her keale vpwards, & to amend it that it might be fitter to carry vs ouer the Sea, for we made full account we had a long troublesom voiage in hád, wherin we might haue many crosses, and wherein we should not be sufficiently prouided, for all things necessarie, although we tooke neuer so much care, and while we were busy about our woske, there came a great Beare vnto vs, wherewith we went into our house, and stood to watch her in our three dores, with harquebushes, and one stood in ordlinancy with a Musket, this Beare came boldlyer vnto vs then euer any had done before, so the came to the neather step she went to one of our dores, and the man that stood in the dore saw her not, because he lookt towards the other dore, but they that stood within saw her, and in great feare called to hun, wherewith he turned about, and although he was in a maze, he shot at her, and the bullet past cleane through her body, whereupon she ran away, yet it was a fearfull thing to see, for the Beare was almost vpon him before he saw her, so that if the peece had failed to giue fire, (as often times they doe) it had cost him his life, and it may be the Beare would haue gotte into the house: the Beare being gone somewhat from the house lay downe, wherewith we went all armed and killed her out-right, and when we had slipt open her belly: we found a peece of a Bucke therein with haire skin and all, which not long before, she had torne and devoured.

The 30. of May, it was indifferent faire weather, but very cold and close aire, the wind West, then we began to set our selues to worke about the boate to amend it, the rest staying in the house to make the sailes and all other things ready, that were necessarie for vs, but while we were busie working at our boate, there ran a Beare vnto vs, wherewith we were forced to leaue worke, but she was shot by our men, then we brake downe the plankes of the roofe of our house, to amend our boate withall, and so proceeded in our worke as well as we could, for euery man was willing to labour, (for we had sore longed for it) and did

more

moze then we were able to doe.

The 31. of May, it was faire weather, but fomewhat colder then befoze, the wind being fouth-weft, whereby the Ice dzaw away, and we wzought hard about our boate, but when we were in the chiefeft part of wozke, there came an other Beare, as if they had fmelt that we would be gone, and that therefoze they defired to taft a péece of fome of vs, foz that was the third day, one after the other, that they fet fo fiercely vpon vs, fo that we were fozced to leaue our wozke and goe into the houfe, and fhe followed vs, but we ftod with our péeces to watch her, and fhot thrée péeces at her, two from our dozes, ¢ one out of the chimney, which all thrée hit her, whereby fhe fared as the Dogge did with the pudding, but her death did vs moze hurt then her life, foz after we ript her belly, we dzeft her liuer and eate it, which in the tafte liked vs well, but it made vs all ficke, fpecially thrée that were excéeding ficke, and we verily thought that we fhould haue loft them, foz all their skins came of, from the fote to the head, but yet they recouered againe, foz the which we gaue God heartic thankes, foz if as then we had loft thefe thrée men, it was a hundzed to one, that we fhould neuer haue gotten from thence, becaufe we fhould haue had too few men to dzaw and lift at our néede.

The 1. of June, it was faire weather, and then our men were foz the moft part ficke with eating the liuer of a Beare, as it is faid befoze, whereby that day there was nothing done about the boate, and then there hung a pot ftill ouer the fire with fome of the liuer in it, but the mafter toke it, and caft it out of the doze, foz we had enough of the fawce thereof: that day foure of our men, that were the beft in health went to the fhip, to fée if there was any thing in it, that would ferue vs in our voiage, and there found a barrell with gép, which we fhared amongft our men, whereof euery one had two, and it did vs great pleafure.

The 2. of June, in the mozning it was faire weather, with a fouth-weft wind, and then fixe of vs went to fé and finde out the beft way, foz vs to bzing our boate and our Scute to the water fide, foz as then the Ice laie fo high and fo thicke one vpon the other, that it fémed vnpoffible to dzaw, oz get our boate and the Scute ouer the Ice, and the fhozteft and beft way that we could find was ftraight from the ship to the water fide, although it was full of hilles and altogether vneuen, and would be great labour and trouble vnto vs but because of the fhortnesse, we efteemed it to be the beft way for vs.

The 3 of June, in the morning it was faire cleare weather the wind Weft, and the ice were somewhat better, and toke great paines with the boate, that at laft we got it ready, after we had wrought fixe daies vpon it: about euening it began to blow hard, and therewith the water was very open, which put vs in god comfort that our deliuerance would fone follow, & that we should once get out of that defolate, and fearefull place.

The 4. of June, it was faire cléere weather, and indifferent warme, & about ý South-eaft Sun, eleuen of vs wet to our Scute where it then lay, and drew it to the ship, at which time the labour feemed lighter vnto vs then it did before whé we toke it in hand, & were forced to leaue it off againe. The reafon thereof was the opinion, that we had that the fnow as then lay harder vpon the groud and fo was become ftronger, and it may be that our courages were better, to fée that the time gaue vs open water, and that our hope was that we should get from thence, and fo thrée of our men ftayd by the Scute to build her to our mindes, and for that it was a herring Scute, which are made narrow behind, therefore they fawed it of behinde, and made it abroad fterne. and better to broke the feas: they built it alfo somewhat higher, and dreft it vp as well they could, they reft of our men were busy in the house to make all other things ready for our voiage and that day drew two fleads with vituals. and other gods vnto the ship, that lay about halfe way betwéene the house and the open water, that after they might haue fo much ý fhorter way, to carry the gods vnto ý water fide, when we should goe away: at which time al the labour and paines that we toke feemed light and eafie vnto vs, because of the hope that we had to get out of that wild defart, irkefome fearefull, and cold rountry.

The 5 of June it was foule weather, with great ftore of haile and fnow, the wind Weft, which made an open water, but as then we could doe nothing without the house, but within we made all things ready, as failes, oares, maftes, fprit, rother, fwerd, and all other neceffarie things.

The

The 6. of June, in the mozning it was faire weather, the wind nozth-eaſt, then we went without Carpenters to the ſhip, to build vp our Scute, and carried two ſleades-full of goods into the ſhip, both victualles and marchandiſe, with other things, which we ment to take with vs; after that there roſe very foule weather in the ſouth-weſt, with ſnow, haile, and raine, which we in long time had not had, whereby the Carpenters were fozced to leaue their wozke, and goe home to the houſe with vs, where alſo we could not be dzie, becauſe we had taken of the deales, therewith to amend our boate & our Scute, there laie but a ſaile ouer it, which would not hold out the water, and the way that laie full of ſnow began to be ſoft, ſo that we left of our ſhoes made of rugge & felt, andp ut on our lether ſhoes.

The 7. of June, there blew a great nozth-eaſt wind, whereby we ſaw the Ice come dziuing in againe, but the Sunne being ſouth-eaſt it was faire weather againe, and then the Carpenters went to the Scute againe to make an end of their wozke, and we packed the marchants goods that we ment to take with vs, and made defences foz our ſelues of the ſaid packes to ſaue vs from the Sea in the open Scute.

The 8. of June, it was faire weather, and we dzew the wares to the ſhip, which we had packed and made ready, and the Carpenters made ready the Scute, ſo that the ſame euening it was almoſt done, the ſame day all our men went to dzaw our boate to the ſhip, and made ropes to dzaw withall, ſuch as we vſe to dzaw with in Scutes, which we caſt ouer our ſhoulders, and held faſt withall our hands, and ſo dzew both with our hands and our ſhoulders, which gaue vs moze fozce, and ſpecially the deſire and great pleaſure we toke to wozke at that time, made vs ſtronger, ſo that we did moze then, then at other times we ſhould haue done, foz that god will on the one ſide, and hope on the other ſide, encreaſed our ſtrenght.

The 9. of June, it was faire weather, with variable windes, then we waſht our ſhirts, and all our linnen, againſt we ſhould be ready to ſaile away, and the Carpenters were ſtill buſie to make an end of the boate and the Scute.

The 10. of June, we caried foure ſleades of goods into the ſhip, the wind then being va riable, and at euening it was noztherly,

D.   and

and we were busie in the house to make all things ready, the wine that was left we put into litle veffels, that fo we might deuide it into both our veffels, and that as we were inclofed by the Ice, (which we well knew would happen vnto vs)we might the eafelier caft the goods vpon the Ice, both out and into the Scutes, as time and place ferued vs.

The 11. of June, it was foule weather, and it blew hard north north-weft, fo that all that day we could doe nothing, and we were in great feare leaft the ftorme would carry the Ice and the fhip both away together, (which might well haue come to paffe)the we fhould haue béene in greater miferie then euer we were,for that our goods both victualles and others were then all in the fhip, but God prouided fo well for vs, that it fell not out fo vnfortunatly.

The 12. of June, it was indifferent faire weather, then we went with hatchets, halberds, fhouels and others inftruments, to make the way plaine, where we fhould draw the Scute and the boate to the water fide, along the way that lay full of knobbes and hilles of Ice, where we wrought fore, with our hatchets & others inftrumens, and while we were in the chiefeft of our worke there came a great leane Beare out of the Sea, vpon the Ice towards vs, which we iudged to come out of Tartaria, for we had féene of them twenty or thirty miles within the fea, & for that we had no muskets, but only one which, our Surgian carried, I ran in great hafte towars the fhip to fetch one or two, which the Beare perceauing ran after me, and was very likely to haue ouertaken me, but our company féeing that, left their workes and ran after her, which made the Beare turne towards them and left me, but when fhe ran towards them, fhe was fhot into the body by the Surgian, and ran away, but becaufe the Ice was fo vneuen and hilly fhe could not go farre, but being by vs ouer taken we killed her out right, and fmot her théeth out of her head, while fhe was yet liuing.

The 13. of June, it was faire weather, then the Maifter and the Carpenter went to the, fhip & there made the Scute & the boate ready, fo that there refted nothing as then, but onely to bring it downe to the water fide, the Maifter and thofe that were with him, féeing that it was open water, and a good Weft wind, came

backs

backe to the house againe, and there he spake vnto William Barents (that had bin long sicke) and shewed him, that he thought it good, (seeing it was a fit time) to goe from thence, and so willed the company to driue the boate and the Scute downe to the water side, and in the name of God to begin our vaiage, to saile from Noua Zembla then William Barents wrote a letter, which he put into a Muskets charge, and hanged it vp in the chimney, shewing how he came out of Holland, to saile to the kindome of China, and what had happ-ned vnto vs, being there on land, with alour crosses, that if any man chanced to come theither, they might know what had happ-ned vnto vs, and how we had bin forced in our extremity to make that house, and had dwelt 10 mounth therein, and for that we were to put to sea in two small ope boates, & to vndertake a dange-rous, & aduenterous voiage in hand, the waister wrote two let-ters, which most of vs subscribed vnto, signifiing, how we had stayed there vpon the land in great trouble and miserie, in hop that our ship would be freed from the Ice, and that we should saile a-way with it againe, and how it fell out to the contrary, and that the ship lay fast in the Ice, so that in the end the time passing away and our victuals beginning to faile vs, we were forced for the sa-ing of our owne liues, to leaue the ship, and to saile away in our open boates, and so to commit our selues into the hands of God. Which done he put into each of our Scutes a letter, y if we chan-ced to loose one another, or y by stormes or any other misaduen-ture we hapened to be cast away, that then by the scute that esca-ped men might know, how we left each other, and so hauing fini-shed all things as we determined, we drew the boate to the water side, and left a man in it, and went and fetcht the Scute, and after that eleuen sleads with goods, as victuals, and some wine that yet remained, and the Marchants woods, which we preserued as wel as we could, viz. 6 packs with fine wollen cloth, a chest with lin-nen, two packets ro Veluet, two smal chests with mony, two dri-fats with the mens clothes, and other things, 13 barrels of bread, a barrell of cheese, a sletch of Bacon, two runlets of oyle, 6. small runlets of wine, two runlets of vineger, with other packs belon-ging to y sailers, so that when they lay al together vpon a heape, a man would haue iudged that they would not haue gon into the Scutes, which being all put into them, we went to the house, and first drew William Barents opon a slead, to the place where our

hauing

hauing bin long sicke, & so we entred into the Scutes, and deuided our selues, into each of them alike, and put into either of them a sicke man, then the Maister caused both the Scutes to ly close one by the other, and there we subcribed to the letters which he had written, the coppie whereof hereafter ensueth, and so committing our selues to the willand merice of God, with a West North-west an endifferent open water, we set saile and put to sea.

The coppie of their letter.

Hauing till this day stayd for the time and opportunity, in hope to get our ship loase, and now are cleane out of hope thereof, for that it lyeth fast shut vp and inclosed in the Ice, and in the last of March, and the first of Aprill, the Ice did so mightily gather toge-ther in great hils, that we could not deuise how to get our Scute and boate into the water, or where to find a conuenient place for it, and for that it seemed almost impossible to get the ship out of the Ice, therefore I and *William Barents* our pilot, and other the officers, & company of Sailors therunto belonging, considering with our selus which would be the best course for vs, to saue our owne liues, and some wares belonging to the Marchanst, we could find no better meanes, thē to mend our boate and Scute and to prouide our selues as well as we could of all things necessarie, that being ready, we might not loose or ouerslip any fit time and opportunity, that God should send vs, for that it stood vs vpon to take the fittest time, o-therewise we should shurely haue perished with hunger and cold, which as yet is to be feared, will goe hard inough with vs, for that there are three or foure of vs that are not able to stirre to doe any thinge, and the best and strongest of vs are so weake, with the great cold and disseases that we haue so long time endured, that we haue but halfe a mans strength, and it is to be feared, that it will ra-ther be worse then better, in regrad of the long voiage that we haue in hand, and our bread, wil not last vs longer then to the end of the Mounth of August, and it may easily fal out, that the voiage being contrary and crosse vnto vs, that before that time we shall not be a-ble to get to any land, where we may procure any victuals or other prouisions for our selues as we haue heatherto done our best, there fore we though it our best course not stay any longer here, for

that

by nature we are bound to seeke our owne good and securites, and so we determined hereupon, and haue vnder written this present letter with our owne hands, vpon the first of Iune 1597. and while vpon the same day we were ready and had a West wind and an indifferent open sea, we did in Gods name prepare our selues, and entred into our voiage, the ship lying as fast as euer it did inclosed in the Ice, notwithstanding that while we were making ready to be gon, we had great wind out of the West North, and North-west, & yet find no alteration nor bettering in the wether, and therefore in the last extremity, we left it. vpon the 13 of Iune.

Iacob hemskerke, Peter Peterson vos, Mr. Hans vos, Laurence Willinson, Peter coruelison, Iohn Remarson, William Baréts, Gerrat de weer, Leonard Hendrickson, Iacob Ionson Scheadam, Iacob Ionsō Strenburger.

The 14. of Iune in the morning, the Sunne easterly, we put off from the land Noua of Zembla, and the fast Ice therunto adioyning, with our boate and our Scute, hauing a West wind, and sailed east-north-east, all that day to the Ilands point., which was fiue miles. but our first beginning was not very good, for we entered fast into the Ice againe, which there laie very hard and fast, which put vs into no small feare and trouble, and being there, foure on vs wēt ofland, to know the scituation thereof, and there we toke many birds which we kild with stones vpon the cliftes.

The 15. of Iune, the Ice began to goe away, then we put to saile againe with a south wind, and past along by the head point, and the fishiungers point, stretching most north-east, and after that North, to the point of desire, which is about 13. miles, and there we laie till the 16. of Iune.

The 16. of Iune, we set saile againe, and got to the Iland of Orange, with a South wind, which is 8. miles distant from the point of desire, there we went one land with two small barrels, & a kettle, to melt snow, & to put ye water into ye barrels, as also to seeke for birds & egges to make meate for our sicke men, and being there, we made fire with such wood as we found there, and melted the snowe, but found no birds, but three of our men went ouer the Ice to the other Iland, and got three birds, and as we came backe againe, our Maister (which was one of the three) fell into

the

the Ice, where he was in great danger of his life, for in that place there ran a great streame, but by Gods helpe he got out againe and came to vs, and there dryed himselfe by the fire that we had made, at which fire we drest the birds, and carried them to the Scute, to our sicke men, and filled our two runlets with water that held about eight gallons a péece, which done we put to the sea againe, with a South-east wind, and drowsie miseling weather, whereby we were all dankish & wet, for we had no shelter in our opē Scutes and sailed West, and West and by South, to the Ice point, and being there, both our Scutes lying hard by each other, the maister called to William Barents, to know how he did, and William Barents made answeare and said, well God be thanked, and I hope before we get to Warehouse, to be able to goe, then he spake to me and said, Gerrit are we about the Ice point? if we be then I pray you lift me vp, for I must veiw it once againe, at which time we had sailed from the Island of Orange to the Ice point, about fiue miles, and then the wind was Westerly, and we made our Scuts fast to a great péece of Ice, and there eate Somewhat, but the weather was still fouler and fouler, so that we were once againe inclosed with Ice, and forced to stay there.

The 17. of Iune in the morning, when we had broken our fastes, the Ice came so fast vpon vs, that it made our haires stare vpright vpon our heades, it was so fearefull to behold, by which meanes we could not make fast our Scutes, so that we thought verily, that it was a foreshowing of our last end, for we draue away so hard with the Ice, and were so sore prest betwéen a flake of Ice, that we thought verily the Scutes would burst in a hundreth péeces, which made vs looke pittifully one vpon the other, for no counsell nor aduise was to be found, but euery minute of an houre, we saw death before our eies, at last being in this discomfort, & extréeme necessity, ȳ maister said if we could take hould with a rope vpon the fast Ice, we might therewith, drawe ȳ Scute vp, and so get it out of the great drift of Ice, but as this counsell was good, yet it was so full of daunger that it was the hassard of his life that should take vpon him to doe it, & with out doing it was it most certaine, ȳ it would cost vs all our liues: this cousell as I said was good, but no man (like to the taile of the mise) durst hang the bell about ȳ cats necke, fearing to be drowned, yet necess-

necessity required to haue it done, and the most danger made vs chuse the least, so that being in that perplexity, I being the light-est of all our company, tooke on me to fasten a rope vpon the fast Ice, and so creeping from one péece of driuing Ice to another, by Gods help got to the fast Ice, where I made a rope fast to a high bowell, and they that were in the Scute, drew it there-by vnto the said fast Ice, and then one man alone could drawe more then all of them could haue done before, and when we had gotten theither, in al haste we tooke our sicke men out and layd them vpon the Ice, laying clothes and other things vnder them, and then tooke all our goods out of the Scutes, and so drew them vpon the Ice, whereby for that time we were deliuered from that great danger, making account that we had escaped out of deaths clawes, as it was most true.

The 18. of June, we repaired and amended our Scutes againe, being much brused and crushed with the racking of the Ice, and were forced to driue all the nailes fast againe, and to péece many things about them, God sending vs wood, wherewith we moult our pitch, and did all other things that belonged thereunto, that done, some of vs went vpon the land, to séeke for egges, which the sicke men longed for, but we could finde none, but we found foure birds, not without great danger of our liues, betwéene the Ice and the firme land, wherein we often fell, and were in no small danger.

The 19. of June, it was indifferent weather, the wind north-west, and west south-west, but we were still shut vp in the Ice, and saw no opening, which made vs thinke that there would be our last aboade, and that we should neuer get from thence, but on the other side we comforted our selues againe, that séeing God had helped vs often times vnexpectedly, in many perils, and that his arme as yet was not shortened, but that he could helpe vp, at his good will and pleasure, it made vs somewat comforta-ble, and caused vs to speake cherefully one vnto the other.

The 20. of June, it was indifferent weather, the wind West, and when the Sunne was south-east, Claes Adrianson, began to be extreeme sicke, wherebe we perceaued that he would not liue long, and the Boateson came into our Scute, and told vs in what case he was, and that he could not long continue aliue,

whereupon

whereupon William Barents speake & said, I thinke I shal not liue longafter him, yet we did not iudge William Barēts to be so sicke, for we sat talking one with the other, and spake of many things, and William Barents read in my Card, which I had made touching our voiage, at last he laid away the Card, and spake vnto me saying Gerrit giue me some drinke, & he had no sooner drunke, but he was taken with so sodain a qualme, that he turned his eies in his head, and died presently, and we had no time to call the maister, out of the Scute, to speake vnto him, and so he died before Claes Adrianson: the death of Willam Barents put vs in no small discomfort, as being the chiefe guide, and onely Pilot on whom we reposed our selues, next vnder God, but we could not striue against God, and therefore we must offorce be content.

The 21. of June, the Ice began to driue away againe, and God made vs some opening with a south-south-west wind, and when the Sunne was north-west, the wind began to blow south-east, with a good gale, and we began to make preparation, to goe from thence.

The 22. of June, in the morning, it blew a good gale out of the south east, and then the Sea was reasonable open, but we were forced to draw our Scutes ouer the Ice, to get vnto it, which was great paine and labour vnto vs; for first we were forced to draw our Scutes ouer a péece of Ice, of 50. paces long, and there put them into the water, and then againe to draw them vp vpon other Ice, and after drew them at the least 100. paces more ouer the Ice, before we could bring them to a good place, where we might easily get out, and being gotten vnto the open water, we committed our selues to God, and set saile, the Sunne being about east-north-east, with an indifferent gale of wind, out of the south, and south-south-east, and sailed west, and west and by south, till the Sunne was south, and then we were round about enclosed with Ice againe, and could not get out, but were forced to lie still, but not long after, the Ice opened againe, like to a sluce, and we past through it and set saile againe, and so sailed along by the land, but were presently enclosed with Ice, but being in hope of opening againe, meane time we eate soms what, for the Ice went not away as it did before: after that we tried all the meanes we could to breake it, but all in vaine,

and

and yet a good while after, the Ice opened againe, and we got out, and sailed along by the land, west and by south, with a south wind.

The 23. of June, we sailed still forewards west and by south, till the Sunne was south-east, and got to the Trust point, which is distant from the Ice point 25. miles, and then could goe no further, because the Ice laie so hard, and so close together, and yet it was faire weather: the same day we tooke the higth of the Sunne with the Astrolabium, and also with our Astronomicall ring, and found his higth to be 37. degrees, and his declination 23. degrees, and 30. minutes, which taken from the higth aforesaid, there rested 13. degrees and 30. minutes, which substracted out of 90. degrees, the higth of the Pole was 76. degrees and 30. minutes, and it was faire Sunne-shine weather, and yet it was not so strong as to melt the snow, that we might haue water to drinke, so that we set all our tin platers and other things ful of snow to melt, and so molt it, and put snow in our mouthes, to melt it downe into our throates, but all was not enough, so that we were compelled to endure great thirst.

The stretching of the land from the house where we wintered, along by the north side of *Noua Zembla*, to the straights of *VVeigats*, where we past ouer to the coast of *Russia*, and ouer the entrie of the white Sea to *Cola*, according to the Card here ensueing.

FRom the low land, to the Streame Baie, the course east and west: 4. miles.

From the Streame Baie, to the Ice hauen point, the course east and by north 3. miles.

From the Ice hauen point, to the Ilands point, the course east north-east 5. miles.

From the Ilands point, to the Flushingers point, the course north-east and by east 3. miles.

From the Flushingers point, to y̌ head point, the course north-east 4. miles.

From the head point, to the point of desire, the course south, and north 6. miles.

From the point of Desire, to the Iland of Orange, north-west 8. miles.

Y

From

From the Islands of Orange, to the Ice point, the course west, and west and by south 5. miles.

From the Ice point, to the point of Thrust, the course west, and by south 25. miles.

From the point of Trust, to Passawes point, the course west, and west and by north 10. miles.

From the Passawe point, to the east end of the crosse Island, the course west and by north 8. miles.

From the east end of the crosse Island, to Williams Iland, the course west and by south 3. miles.

From Williams Island, to the black point, the course West South-west, 6. miles.

From the black point, to the east end of the admirable Island, the course West South-west 7. miles.

From the east to the west point of the admirable Island, the course west southwest 5 miles.

From the West point of the admirable Island, to Cape Planto, the course South-west and by west, 10. miles.

From Cape de Planto, to Lombs-bay, the course west South-west, 8. miles.

From Lombsbay to the Staues point, the course west South-west 10. miles.

From the Staues point to Langenesse, the course South-west & by South, 14. miles.

From Langenes to Cape de Cant, the course South-west and by South 6. miles.

From Cape de Cant, to the point with the black cliffes, the course South and by west, 4. miles.

From the point with the black cliffes, to the black Island, the course South south east 3. miles.

From the black Island, to Constint-sarke, the course east and west 2 miles.

From constint sarke, to the Crosse point, the course South south east 5 miles.

From crosse point, to S. Laurence bay, the course South south east 6 miles.

From S. Laurence bay, to Delshauen, the course South east 6. miles.

From

From Mel-hauen to the two Iſlands, the courſe South South-eaſt 16.miles.

From the 2.Iſlands, where we croſt ouer to the Ruſſia coaſt,to the Iſlands of Matſlw and delgoye, the courſe South-weſt 30. myles.

From Matſlw & delgoye, to the crééke where we ſailed the compaſſe round about,and came to the ſame place againe. 22 miles.

From that crééke to Colgoy, the courſe Weſt No2th-weſt, 18. miles.

From Colgoy to the eaſt point of Camdenas, the courſe Weſt No2th-weſt, 20. miles.

From the Eaſt point of Camdenas, to the Weſt ſide of the White ſea, the courſe Weſt No2th-weſt, 40 miles.

From the Weſt point of the White ſea, to the 7.Iſlands, the courſe No2th-weſt, 14.miles.

From the 7.Iſlands, to the Weſt end of Kilduin, the courſe No2th-weſt, 20.miles.

From the weſt end of Kelduin, to the place where Iohn Cornelis came vnto vs, the courſe No2th-weſt and by Weſt, 7.miles.

From thence to Cola, the courſe Weſt Southerly 18.miles.

So that we ſailed in the two open Scutes, ſome times in the Ice, then ouer the Ice, and th2ough the ſea, 381 miles flemiſh, which is 1143 miles Jngliſh.

The 24.of Iune the Sunne being Eaſterly, we rowed here and there in the Ice, to ſe where we might beſt goe out, but we ſaw no opening, but when the Sunne was South, we got into the ſea, fo2 the which we thanked God moſt heartilie, that he had ſent vs an vnerpected opening, and then we ſailed with an Eaſt wind, and went luſtily fo2ward, ſo that we made our account to get aboue the point of Naſſawes cloſe by the land, & we could eaſily ſée the point of Naſſawes, and made our account to be about 3 miles from it, the wind being South and South South-weſt, then ſire of our men went on land, and there found ſome wood, whereof they b2ought as much as they could into the Scutes, but found neither birds no2 egges, with the which wood they ſod a pot of water pap, (which we called Matſammo2e) that we might eate ſome warme thing the wind blowing ſtil Southerly.

The 25.of Iune, it blew a great South-wind, and the Ice

whereunto we made our selues fast; was not very strong, whereby we were in great feare, that we should breake off from it, and
driue into the sea, for when the Sun was in the West, a péece of
that Ice brake of, whereby we were forced to dislodge, and make
our selues fast to another péece of Ice.

The 26. of June, it still blew hard out of the South, and broke
the Ice whereunto we were fast, in péeces, and we thereby draue
into the sea, and could get no more to the fast Ice, whereby we
were in a thousand dangers to be all cast away, and driuing in the
fort in the sea, we rowed as much as we could, but we could not
get néere vnto the land, therefore we hoysed vp our fock, and so
made vp with our saile, but our fock-mast brake, twice in péeces,
and then it was worse for vs then before, and notwithstanding
that there blew a great gale of wind, yet we were forced to hoyse
vp our great saile, but the wind blew so hard into it, that if we had
not presently taken it in againe, we had sunke in the sea, or else our
boate would haue bin filled with water, for the water began, to
leap ouer borde, and we were a good way in the sea, at which time
the waues went so hollow, that it was most fearful, and we ther-
by saw nothing, but death before our eyes, and euery twinckling
of an eyelowkt when we should sincke. But God that had deliuered
vs out of so many dangers of death, holpe vs once againe, & contrary to our expectations, sent vs a North-west wind, and so with
great danger we got to the fast Ice againe, when we were deliuered
out of that danger, and knew not where our other Scute was, we
sailed one mile along by the fast Ice, but found it not, whereby we
were wholy out of heart, & in great feare the they were drowned, at
which time it was mistie weather, and so sailing along, & hearing
no newes of our other scute, we shot of a Musket, which they hearing
shot of another but yet we could not sée each other, meane time ap-
proching néerer to each other, & the weather waring somwhat cléer-
rer, as we & they shot once againe, we saw the smoake of their péece,
& at last we met together againe, & saw thē ly fast betwéen driuing
& fast Ice, & when we got néere vnto thē, we went ouer the Ice, &
holp them to vnlade the goods out of their Scute, and drew it ouer
the Ice, and with much paine and trouble brought it into the open
water againe, and while they were fast in the Ice, we found some
wood vpon the land, by the sea side, and when we lay by each other
we sod some bread and water together, and eate it vp warme,
which

which did vs much good.

The 17. of June, we ſet ſaile with an indifferent gale out of the eaſt, & got a mile aboue the Cape de Naſſaw, one the weſt ſide thereof, and then we had the wind againſt vs, and we were for-red to take in our ſailes, and began to rowe and as we went along cloſe by the land, we ſaw ſo many Sea-horſes lying vpon the Ice, that it was admirable, and a great number of birds, at the which we diſcharged 2. muſkets and killed twelue of thē, which we fetcht into our Scutes, and rowing in that ſort, we had a great miſt, and then we entred into driuing Ice, ſo that we were compelled to make our Scutes faſt vnto the faſt Ice, and to ſtay there till the weather brake vp, the wind being weſt north-weſt, and right againſt vs.

The 28. of June, when the Sunne was in the eaſt, we laid all our goods vpon the Ice, and then drew the Scutes vpon the Ice alſo, becauſe we were ſo hardly preſt on all ſides, with the Ice, and the wind came out of the Sea vpon the land, and therefore we were in feare to be wholely incloſed with the Ice, and ſhould not be able to get out thereof againe, and being vpon the Ice, we laid ſailes ouer our Scutes, and laie downe to reſt, appointing one of our men to kéepe watch, and when the Sunne was north there came thrée Beares towards our Scutes, wherewith he that kept the watch cried, thrée Beares thrée Beares, at which noiſe we leapt out of our boates, with our muſkets, that were laden with haile-ſhot, to ſhoote at birds, and had no time to diſcharge them, and therefore ſhot at them therewith, and although that kinde of ſhot could not hurt them much, yet they ranne away, and in the meane time they gaue vs leiſure to lade our muſkets with bullets, and by that meanes we ſhot one of the thrée, dead, which the other two perceauing ranne away, but within two houres after they came againe, but when they were almoſt at vs, and heard vs make a noiſe, they ranne away, at which time the wind was weſt and weſt and by north, which made the Ice driue with great force into the eaſt.

The 29. of June, the Sunne being ſouth-ſouth-weſt, the two Beares came againe to the place where the dead Beare lais, where one of them tooke the dead Beare in his mouth, and went a great way with it ouer the rugged Ice, & then began to eate it,

R 3   which

which we perceauing shot a musket at her, but she hearing the noise thereof, ran away, and let the dead Beare lie, then foure of vs went thither, and saw that in so shozt a time she had eaten almost the halfe of her, we tooke the dead Beare and laid it vpon a high heape of Ice, that we might see it out of our Scute, that if the Beare came againe we might shot at her, at which time we tried the great strenght of the Beare, that carried the dead Beare as lightely in her mouth, as if it had beene nothing, where as we foure had enough to doe to cary away the halfe dead Beare betweene vs, then the wind still held west, which dzaue the Ice into the east.

The 30. of June, in the mozning, when the Sunne was east and by nozth, the Ice dzaue hard east-ward, by meanes of the west wind, and then there came two Beares vpon a peece of Ice that dzaue in the Sea, and thought to set vpon vs, and made show as if they would leape into the water, and come to vs, but did nothing, whereby we were of opinion, that they were the same Beares, that had beene there befoze, and about the south-south-east Sunne, there came an other Beare vpon the fast Ice, and made towards vs, but being neare vs, and hearing vs make a noise, she went away againe, then the wind was west-south-west, and the Ice began somewhat to falle from the land, but because it was mistie weather, and a hard wind, we durst not put to Sea, but staied foz a better oppoztunitie.

The 1. of Julie, it was indifferent faire weather, with a west-nozth-west wind, and in the mozning the sunne being east, there came a beare from the dziuing yce towards vs, and swam ouer the water to the fast yce whereon we lay, but when she heard vs, she came no nearer, but ran away, and when the sunne was south-east, the Ice came so fast in towards vs, that all the Ice whereon we lay with our Scutes and our goods, brake and ran one peece vpon another, whereby we were in no small feare, foz at that time most of our goods fell into the water, but we with great diligence dzew our Scutes further vpon the Ice towards the land, where we thought to bebetter defended from the dziuing of the Ice, and as we went to fetch our goods, we fell into the greatest trouble that euer we had befoze, foz y we endured so great danger in the sauing thereof, that as we laid hold vpon on peece thereof, the rest sunke

downe

downe with the Ice, and many times the Ice brake vnder our owne féet, whereby we were wholy discomforted, and in a maner cleane out of all hope, expecting no issue thereof, in such sort that our trouble at that time surmounted all our former cares and impeachments, and when we thought to draw vp our boates vpon the Ice, the Ice brake vnder vs, and we were caried away with the Scute, and al by the driuing Ice, and when we thought to saue the goods, the Ice brake vnder our féet, and with that the Scute brak in many places, especially ý which we had méded, as ý mast, ý mast planke, and almost al the Scute, wherein one of our men that was sicke, and a chest of mony lay, which we with great danger of our liues got out from it, for as we were doing it, the Ice that was vnder our féet draue from vs, and slid vpon other Ice, whereby we were in danger to burst both our armes ꝫ our legs, at which time thinking, ý we hadbin cleane quit of our Scute, we beheld each other in pittiful maner, knowing not what we should doe, our liues depending thereon, but God made so good prouission for vs, ý ý péeces of Ice draue from each other, wherewith we ran in great haste vnto the Scute, and drew it to vs again in such case as it was, and layd it vpon the fast Ice by the boate, where it was in more security, which put vs vnto an excéeding and great and dangerous labor, from the time that the Sunne was south east, vntill it was West South west, and in al that time we rested not, which made vs extreame weary, and wholy out of comfort, for that it troubled vs sore, and it was much more fearfull vnto vs, then at that time when William Barents dyed, for there we were almost drowned, ꝫ that day we lost (which was sunke in the sea) two barrels of bread, a chest with linné cloth, a driefat with the Sailors clothes, our Astronicale ring, a pack of Scarlet-cloth, a runlet of oyle, ꝫ some chéeses and a runlet of wine, which bongd with the Ice, so that there was not any thing thereof saued.

The 2. of Julie, the sunne East, there came another beare vnto vs, but we making a noyse she ran away, and when the Sun was West South-west, it began to be faire weather, then we began to mend our Scute, with the planks wherewith we had made the buyckmith, and while 6. of vs were busied about mending of our Scute the other sixe went further into the land, to séeke for some wood, and to fetch some stones, to lay vpon the Ice, that we might

make

make a fire thereon, therewith to melt our pitch, which we should need about the Scute, as also to see if they could fetch any wood for a mast, which they found with certaine staues, and brought them where the Scutes lay, and when they came to vs againe, they shewed vs that they had found certaine wood that had bin clouen, & brought some wedges with them, wherwith the said wood had bin cloue, whereby it appeared that men had bin there, then we made al the haste we could to make a fire and to melt our pitch, and to do al other things that were necessary to be done for the repairing of our Scute, so that we got it ready againe, by that the Sunne was North-east, at which time also we rosted our birds, & made a good meale with them.

The 3. of July, in the morning the Sunne being East, two of our men went to the water, and there they found two of our oares our helme stickes, the pack of Scarlet cloth, the chest with linnen cloth, and a hat that fell out of the oriefat, whereby we gest, that it was broken in peeces, which they perceiuing, tooke as much with them as they could carry, and came vnto vs, shewing vs that they had left more goods behind them, whereupon the Maister with 5. more of vs went thither, & drew al the goods vpon the firme Ice, y when we went away, we might take it with vs; but they could not carry the chest nor the pack of cloth (that were ful of water) because of their waight, but were forced to let them stand, till we went away, that the water might drop out of them, and so they did, the Sunne being South west: there came another great beare vnto vs, which the man that kept watch saw not, and had béene denoured by her, if one of our other men that lay downe in the ship, had not espied her, and called to him that kept watch, to looke to himselfe, who therewith ran away, meane time the beare was shot into the body, but she escaped, and that time the wind was east, north-east.

The 4. of July it was so faire cleare weather, that from the time we were first in Noua Zembla, we had not the like, then wee washt the veluets that had béene wet with the salt water, in fresh water, drawne out of snow and then dryed them, and packt them vp againe, at which time the wind was west, & west southwest.

The 5. of July it was faire weather, the wind west, southwest,

the

the ſame day dyed Iohn Franſon of Harlem (Claes Adrians ne∗ phew, that dyed the ſame day when William Barents dyed) the Sunne being then about ₱orth, north∗weſt, at which time the Ice came mightily driuing in vpon vs, and then ſixe of our men went into the land, and there fetcht ſome fire∗wood to dreſſe our meate.

The 6. of Iuly it was miſty weather, but about euening it be∗ gan to clére vp, and the wind was ſouth∗eaſt, which put vs in ſome comfort, and yet we lay faſt vpon the Ice.

The 7. of Iuly it was faire weather with ſome raine, the wind weſt, South∗weſt, and at euening weſt, and by north, then wée went to the open water, and there killed thirtéene birds, which we toke vppon a péece of driuing Ice, and layd them vpon the faſt Ice.

The 8. of Iuly it was cloſe miſty weather, then we dreſt the foules which we had killed, which gaue vs a princely mealetide, in the euening there blew a freſh gale of wind, out of the ₱orth eaſt, which put vs in great comfort to get from thence.

The 9. of Iuly in the morning, the Ice began to driue, where∗ by we got open water on the land ſide, and then alſo the faſt Ice whereon we lay, began to driue, whereupon the maſter and ẙ men went to fetch the packe and the cheſt, that ſtood vpon the Ice, to put them into the Scute, and then drew the Scutes to the water, at leaſt 340. paces, which was hard for vs to do, in regard that the labour was great, and we very weake, & when the Sun was ſouth ſouth eaſt we ſet ſaile, with an eaſt wind, but when the ſunne was weſt, we were forced to make towards the faſt Ice a∗ gaine, becauſe thereabouts it was not yet gon, ẙ wind being ſouth, and came right from the land, whereby we were in good hope that it would driue away, and that we ſhould procéede in our voyage.

The 10. of Iuly, from the time that the ſunne was eaſt, north∗ eaſt, till it was eaſt, we toke great paines & labour to get through the Ice, and at laſt we got through, and rowed forth, vntill wée happened to fall betwéene two great flakes of Ice, that cloſed one with the other, ſo that we could not get through, but were forced to draw the Scutes vpon them, and to vnlade the goods, and then to draw them ouer to the open water on the other ſide, and then we muſt go fetch the goods alſo to the ſame place, being at

S

leaſt

leaſt 110. paces long, which was very hard foꝛ vs, but there was no remedy, foꝛ it was but a folly foꝛ vs to thinke of any wearines, and when we were in the open water againe, we rowed foꝛward as well as we could, but we had not rowed long, befoꝛe we fell betwæne two great flakes of Ice, that came dꝛiuing one againſt the other, but by Gods help, and our ſpædy rowing, we got from betwæne them, befoꝛe they cloſed vp, and being thꝛough we had a hard weſt wind, right in our tæth ſo ẏ of foꝛce we were conſtrained to make towards the faſt Ice that lay by the ſhoꝛe, and at laſt with much trouble, we got vnto it, and being there, we thought to row along by the faſt Ice, vnto an Iſland that we ſaw befoꝛe vs, but by reaſon of the hard contrary wind, we could not goe farre, ſo that we were compelled to dꝛaw the Scutes and the gꝏds vpon the Ice, to ſæ what weather God would ſend vs, but our courages were cꝏled, to ſæ our ſelues ſo often incloſed in ẏ Ice being in great feare ẏ by meanes of the long and continuall paines (which we were foꝛced to take) we ſhould lꝏſe all our ſtrength, & by that meanes ſhould not long be able to continue oꝛ hold out.

The 11. of July in the moꝛning as we ſate faſt vpon the Ice, the ſunne being Noꝛth eaſt, there came a great beare out of the water, running towards vs, but we watcht foꝛ her with thꝛæ muſkets, and when ſhe came within 30. paces of vs, we ſhot all the thꝛæ muſkets at her, and killed her outright, ſo that ſhe ſtirred not a fꝏte, and we might ſæ the fat run out at the holes of her ſkinne, that was ſhot in with the muſkets, ſwimme vpon the water like oyle, and ſo dꝛining dead vpon the water, we went vpon a flake of Ice to her, and putting a rope about her neck, dꝛew her vp vpon the Ice, and ſmit out her tæth, at which time we meaſured her body, & found it to be eight fꝏte thick, then we had a weſt winde with cloſe weather, but when the ſunne was South it began to clære vp, then thꝛæ of our men went to the Iſland that lay befoꝛe vs, and being there, they ſaw the Croſſe Iſland, lying weſtward from them, and went thither to ſæ if that ſommer there had bæne any Ruſſian there, and went thither vpon the faſt Ice, that lay betwæne the two Iſlands, and being in the Iſland, they could not perceiue that any man had bæne in it ſince we were there, there they got 70. egges, but when they had them, they knew not wherein to carry them, at laſt one of them
put

put off his breeches, and tying them fast below, they carried them betwéene two of them, and the third bare ths musket: and so came to vs againe, after they had béene twelue houres out, which put vs no small feare to thinke what was become of them, they told vs that they had many times gone vp to the knées in water, vpon the Ice betwéene both the Jslands : and it was at least 6. miles to and fro, that they had gone which made vs wonder how they could indure it, séeing we were all so weake. With the egges that they had brought, we were al wel comforted, and fared like Lords, so that we foond some reliefe in our great misery, and then we shared our last wine amongst vs, whereof euery one had thrée glasses.

The 12. of July in the morning, when the sunne was East, the wind began to blow east, and east north east, with misty weather, and at euening six of our men went into the land, to séeke certaine stones, and found some, but none of the best sort, and comimng backe againe, either of them brought some wood.

The 1?. of July it was a faire day, then seuen of our men went to the firme land, to séeke for more stones, & found some, at which time the wind was South-east.

The 14. of July it was faire weather with a good south wind, and then the Ice began to driue from the land, whereby we were in good hope to haue an open water, but the wind turning wester-ly againe, it lay still when the sunne was south-west, thrée of our men went to the next Iland, that lay before vs, and there shot a Barcheynet, which they brought to the Scute, and gaue it a-mongst vs, for all our goods were common.

The 15. of July, it was misty weather, that morning the wind was south-east, but the sunne being west, it began to raine, and the wind turned west and west south west.

The 16. of July there came a beare from the firme land, that came very néere vnto vs, by reason that it was as white as snow, whereby at first we could not discerne it to be a beare, because it shewed so like the snow, but by her stirring at last wee perceiued her, and as she came néere vnto vs, we shot at her, and hit her, but she ran away : that morning, the wind was west, and after that againe, east north-east with close weather.

The 17. July, about the south south east sunne, 5. of our men

went

went againe to the néerest Island, to sée if there appeared any open water, for our long staying there was no small griefe vnto vs, perceiuing not how we should get from thence, who being halfe way thither, they found a beare lying behind a péece of Ice, which the day before had béene shot by vs, but she hearing vs went away, but one of our men following her with a boate-hooke, thrust her into the skinne, wherewith the beare rose vp vpon her hinder féet, and as the man thrust at her againe, she stroke the Iron of the boat-hooke in péeces, wherewith the man fell downe vpon his buttocks, which our other two men séeing, two of them shot the beare into the body, and with that she ran away, but the other man went after her with his broken staffe, and stroke the beare vpon the backe, wherewith the beare turnd about against the man thrée times one after the other, and then the other two came to her, and shot her into the body againe, wherewith she sat downe vpon her buttocks, and could scant runne any further, and then they shot once againe, wherewith she fell downe, and they snot her téeth out of her head: all that day the wind was north-east, & east north-east.

The 18. of July, about the east sunne, thrée of our men went vp vpon the highest part of the land, to sée if there was any open water in the sea, at which time they saw much open water, but it was so farre from the land, that they were almost out of comfort, because it lay so farre from the land and the fast Ice, being of opinion that we should not be able to drawe the Scutes and the goods so farre thither, because our strengthes stil began to decrease: and the sore labour and paine that we were forced to indure more and more increased, and comming to our Scutes, they brought vs that newes, but we being compelled thereunto by necessity abandoned all wearines and faint heartednes, & determined with our selues to bring the boates and the goods to the water side, and to row vnto that Ice, where we must passe ouer to get to the open water, and when we got to it, we vnladed our scutes, and drewe them first ouer the Ice to the open water, and after that the goods; it being at the least 1000. paces, which was so sore a labour for vs, that as we were in hand therewith we were in a manner ready to leaue off in the middle thereof, and feared that wée should not goe through withall, but for that we had gone through so many dangers,

gers,

gers, we hoped ý we ſhould not be faint therin, wiſhing ý it might
be ý laſt trouble ý we ſhould as then indure, & ſo we great difficultie
got into the open water, about the ſouth-weſt ſunne, then we ſet
ſaile, till the ſunne was weſt and by ſouth; & preſently ſell amongſt
the Jce againe, where we were ſorced to drawe vp the Scutes a-
gaine vpon the Jce, and being vpon it, we could ſée the croſſe J-
ſland, which we geſt to be about a mile from vs, the wind then being eaſt, and eaſt north-eaſt.

The 19. of July lying in that manner vpon the Jce, about the
Eaſt Sunne, ſeuen of our men went to the Croſſe Jſland, and being there they ſaw great ſtore of opē water in ý Weſt, wherewith
they much reioyced, and made as great haſte as they could to get
to the Scutes againe, but before they came away they got a hundred egges, and brought them away with them, and comming to
the Scutes, they ſhewed vs that they had ſéen, as much open water
in the ſea, as they could decerne, being in god hope, that that would
be the laſt time that they ſhould draw the Scutes ouer the Jce,
and that it ſhould be no more meaſured by vs, and in that ſort put
vs in god comfort, whereupon we made ſpéde to dreſſe our egges
& ſhared them amongſt vs, and preſently the Sun being South
South-weſt we ſell to worke, to make all things ready, to bring
the Scutes to the water, which were to be drawen at leaſt 200.
paces ouer the Jce, which we did with a god courage, becauſe we
were in god hope that it would be the laſt time, and getting to the
water, we put to ſea with Gods helpe, with an Eaſt, and Eaſt
North eaſt wind, & a god gale, ſo that with the weſt Sun, we paſt
by the Croſſe Jſland, which is diſtant from Cape de Naſſawes 10.
miles, and preſently after that the Jce left vs, & we got cléere out
of it, yet we ſaw ſome in the ſea, but it troubled vs not and ſo we
held our courſe Weſt and by South, with a god gale of wind out
of the Eaſt, and Eaſt North-eaſt, ſo that we geſt that betwéene
euery meale-tide we ſailed eightéene miles, wherewith we were
excéedingly comforted, giuing God thanks, that he had deliuered vs
out of ſo great and many difficulties, (wherein it ſéemed that we
ſhould haue bin ouerwhelmed,) hoping in his merſie, that from
thence forth he would ayde vs to bring our voyage to an end.

The 20. of July, hauing ſtill a god gale about the South-eaſt
Sunne, we paſt a long by the black point, which is twelue miles

diſtan

diſtant from the croſſe Jſland, and ſailed Weſt South weſt, and
about the euening with the Weſt Sunne, we ſaw the Admirable
Jſland, and about the North Sun paſt a long by it, which is diſtant from the black point eight miles, and paſſing along by it, we
ſaw about two hundred ſea horſes, lying vpon a flake of Jce, and
we ſayled cloſe by them, and draue them from thence, which had
almoſt coſt vs dœre, for they being mighty ſtrong fiſhes, and of
great force, ſwain towards vs, (as if they would be reuenged on
vs for the diſpight that we had don them (round about our Scuts
with a great noyſe, as if they would haue deuoured vs, but we eſ-
caped from them by reaſon, that we had a good gale of wind, yet it
was not wiſely done of vs, to wake ſléeping wolues.

The 21. of July, we paſt by Cape Pluncio, about the Eaſt
North-eaſt Sune, w̃ lyeth Weſt South-weſt ight miles from ȳ
Admirable Jſland, & w̃ the good galeȳ we had about ȳ South-w eſt
Snu, we ſailed by Langenes, 9 miles frõ Cape Pluncio, there ȳ lãd
reacheth moſt South-weſt and we had a good North-eaſt winde.

The 22. of July, we hauing ſo good a gale of wind, when we
came to Cape de Cant, there we went on land to ſéeke for ſome
birds & egs, but we found none, ſo we ſayled forwards, but after ȳ
about ȳ South Sun we ſaw a clift, ȳ was ful of birds, thither we
ſailed & caſting ſtones at them, we killed 22. birds, and got fiftéene
egges, which one of our men fetcht from the clift, and if we would
haue ſtayed there any longer, we might haue taken a hundred or
two hundred birds at leaſt, but becauſe the maiſter was ſomewhat
further into ſea-ward then we, and ſtayed for vs, and for that we
would not looſe that faire fore-wind, we ſailed forwards a long by
the land, and about the South-Weſt Sunne, we came to another
point, where we got a hundred twenty fiue birds, which we tooke
with our hands out of their neaſts, and ſome we killed with ſtones
and made them fal downe into the water, for it is a thing certaine
ȳ thoſe birds neuer vſed to ſée men, & that nom an had euer ſought
or vſed to take them, for elſe they would haue flowne away, and
th it they feared no body but the Foxes and other wilde beaſtes,
that could not clime vp the high clifts, and that therefore they had
made their neſts thereon, where they were out of feare of any
beaſtes camming vnto them, for we were in no ſmall daunger of
breaking of our legges and armes, eſpecially as we came downe
againe

againe, becaufe the clift was fo high and fo ffepe, thofe bids had e-
uery one but one egge in their neaffs, and that lay vpon the bare
clift without any ffraw o2 other thing vnder them, which is to be
wond2ed at, to thinke how they could b2eed thir young ones in fo
great cold, but it is to be thought and beleeued, that they therfo2e
fit but vpon on egge, that fo the heat which they giue in b2eeding fo
many, may be wholy giuen vnto one egge, and by that meanes it
hath all the heat of the birde vnto it felfe, and there alfo we found
many egges, but moff of them were foule and bad, and when we
left them, the wind fell flat againff vs, and blew No2th-weff, and
there alfo we had much Jce, and we toke great paines to get from
the Jce, but we could not get aboue it, and at laff by lauering we
fell into the Jce, and being there we faw much open water towards the land, wherevnto we made as well as we could, but our
Maiffer (that was mo2e to fea ward) perceiuing vs to be in the Jce
thought we had gotten fome hurt, and lauered to and againe along
by the Jce, but at laff feeing that we failed therein, he was of opinion that we faw fome open water, and that we made towards it
(as it was true) and therefo2e he wound alfo towards vs, and came
to land by vs where we found a good hauen, and lay fafe almoff
from all winds, and he came thither about two houres after vs,
there we went on land, and got fome eggs and fome wood to make
a fire, wherewith we made ready the birds that we had taken, at
which time we had a No2th weff wind with clofe weather.

The 23. of July, it was darke and miffie weather, with a No2th
wind, whereby we were fo2ced to lye ffill in that creeke o2 hauen:
meane time fome of our men went on land, to feeke fo2 fome egges
and ffones, but found not many, but a reafonable number of good
ffones.

The 24. of July, it was faire weather, but the wind ffill No2-
therly, whereby we were fo2ced to lye ffill, and about none we
toke the higth of y Sun, with our aftrolabium, and found it to be
eluated aboue the Ho2izon 37. degrees & 20. min. his declination
20. degrees & 10. min. which fubffracted fro y higth afo2efaid reffed
17. degrees & 10 minutes, which taken from 90 degrees, the higth
of the Pole was 73. degrees and 10. minutes, and fo2 y we lay ffil
there, fome of our men went often times on land, to feeke ffones,
and found fome that were as good as euer any that we found.

The

The 25. of Iuly it was darke mifty weather, the wind north, but we were forced to ly ftill, becaufe it blew fo hard.

The 26. of Iuly it began to be faire weather, which we had not had for certaine daies together, the wind ftill north; and about the fouth funne, we put to fea, but it was fo great a créeke that we were forced to put foure miles into the fea, before wée could get about the point thereof: and it was moft in the wind, fo that it was midnight before wee got aboue it, fometimes fayling, and fometimes rowing: and hauing paft it, we ftroke out failes, and rowed along by the land.

The 27. of Iuly it was faire calme weather, fo that we rowed all that day, through the broken Ice, along by the land, the wind being northweft, and at euening about the weft funne, we came to a place where there ran a great ftreame, whereby we thought that we were about Conftinfarke, for we faw a great créeke, and we weree of opinion ÿ it went through to the Tartarian fea, our courfe was moft fouth-weft: about the north funne we paft along by the croffe point, and failed betwéen the firme land and an Ifland, & then went South fouth-eaft, with a Northweft wind and made good fpéed, the maifter with ÿ Scute being a good way before vs, but whé he had gotten about ÿ point of the Ifland, he ftaied for vs, & there we lay by ÿ clifts, hoping to take fome birds, but got none, at which time we had failed from Cape de Cant along by Conftinfarke, to the croffe point 20. miles, our courfe South fouth-eaft, the wind North-weft.

The 28. of Iuly it was faire weather, with a North-eaft wind, then we failed along by the land, and with the South-weft funne, got before S. Laurence Bay, or Sconce point, and fayled South fouth-eaft, 6. miles, and being there, we found two Ruffians Lodgies, or fhips, beyond the point, wherewith we were not a little comforted, to thinke that we were come to the place where we found men, but were in fome doubt of them, becaufe they were fo many, for at that time, wee fawe at leaft 30. men, and knew not what they were, there with much paine and labour, we got to the land, which they perceiuing, left off their worke, and came towards vs, but without any armes, and wée alfo went on fhore, as many as were well, for diuers of vs were very ill at eafe, and weake by reafon of a great fcouring in their

bodyes,

bodies, and when wee met together, wee saluted each other in
friendly wise, they after theirs, and we after our manner, and
when we were met, both they and we lookt each other stedfastly
in the face, for that some of them knew vs, and we them, to bée
the same men which the yeare before, when we paſt through the
Weigats, had béen in our ſhip : at which time we perceiued ŷ they
were abaſht, and wondered at vs, to remember that at that time
we were ſo well furniſhed with a great ſhip, that was excéedingly
prouided of all things neceſſary, and then to ſée vs ſo leane & bare,
& with ſo ſmall Scutes into that country : & amongſt them there
were two, that in friendly manner clapt ŷ maſter & me vpon the
ſhoulder, as knowing vs ſince ŷ voyage: for there was none of all
our men that was as then in that voiage, but we two onley, and
aſked vs for our Crable, meaning our ſhip, and we ſhewed
them by ſignes as well as we could (for we had no interpreter)
that we had loſt our ſhip in the Ice, wherewith they ſayd, Crable
pro pal, (which we vnderſtood to be, haue you loſt your ſhip) and
we made anſwere, Crable pro pal, which was as much as to ſay,
that we had loſt our ſhip, and many more words we could not vſe,
becauſe we vnderſtood not each other, then they made ſhew to be
ſorry for our loſſe, and to be grieued that we the yeare before had
béene there with ſo many ſhips, and then to ſée vs in ſo ſimple mã-
ner, & made vs ſignes that then they had drunke wine in our ſhip,
and aſked vs what drinke we had now, wherewith one of our
men went into the ſcute and drew ſome water, and let them taſte
thereof, but they ſhakt their heads, and ſaid No dobbre (that is,
it is not good) then our maſter went néerer vnto them, and ſhewed
them his mouth, to giue them to vnderſtand that we were troubled with a loſneſſe in our bellies, and to know if they could giue
vs any councel to help it, but they thought we made ſhew that we
had great hunger, wherewith one of them went vnto their longing, and fetcht a round Rie loafe, weighing about 8. pounds, with
ſome ſmored foules, which we accepted thankfully, and gaue them
in exchange halfe a dozen of Muſchuyt, then our maſter led two
of the chiefe of them, with him into his Scute, & gaue them ſome
of the wine that we had, being almoſt a gallon, for it was ſo néere
out: and while we ſtaied there, we were very familiar with them,
and went to the place where they lay, & ſod ſome of our miſchuyt

T   with

with water by their fire, that we might eate some warme thing
downe into our bodies, and we were much comforted to see the
Russians for that in thirtéene moneths time, that wee departed
from Iohn Cornelison, we had not séene any man, but onely monsterous and cruell wild beares: for that as then we were in some
comfort, to sée that we had liued so long, to come in company of
men againe, and therewith we said vnto eath other, now we hope
it will fall out better with vs, séeing we haue found men againe,
thanking God with all our hearts, that he had béene so gracious
and mercifull vnto vs, to giue vs life vntill that time.

The 29. of Iuly it was reasonable faire weather, & that morning
the Russians began to make preparatiō to be gone, & to set saile:
at which time they digd certaine barrels with traine oile out of
the steges, which they had buried there, and put it into their ships,
and we not knowing whither they would go, saw them saile towards ỹ VVeigats: at which time also we set saile, & followed after
them, but they sayling before vs, and we following them, along
by the land, the weather being close and misty, we lost the sight of
them, and knew not whether they put into any créeke, or sayled
forward, but we held on our course, South-south east with a
North-west wind, and then South-east, betwéene two Islands,
vntill we were inclosed with Ice againe, and saw no open water,
whereby we supposed that they were about the VVeigats, and
that the North-west wind had driuen the Ice into that créeke, and
being so inclosed in Ice, & saw no open water before vs, but with
great labour and paines, we went back againe to the two Islands
aforesaid, and there about the North-east sunne, we made our
Scutes fast at one of the Islands, for as then it began to blowe
hard.

The 30. of Iuly lying at anchor, the wind still blew North-
west, with great store of raine, and a sore storme, so that although
we had couered our Scutes with our sailes, yet we could not lye
dry, which was an vnaccustomed thing vnto vs: for we had had
no raine in long time before, and yet we were forced to stay there
all that day.

The 31. of Iuly, in the morning, about the North-east sunne,
we rowed frō that Island to another Island, whereon there stood
two crosses, whereby we thought that some men had laine there
about

about trade of merchandise, as the other Russians that we saw before had done, but we found no man there, the wind as then béeing North-west, whereby the Ice draue still towards the Weigats: there, to our great good, we went on land, for in that Iland, we found great store of Leple leaues, which serued vs excéeding well, and it séemed that God had purposely sent vs thither: for as then we had many sicke men, and most of vs were so troubled with a scouring in our bodies, and were thereby become so weake, that we could hardly row, but by meanes of those leaues, we were healed thereof: for that as soone as we had eaten them, we were presently eased and healed, whereat we could not choose but wonder, & therefore we gaue God great thanks, for that, and for many other his mercies shewed vnto vs, by his great and vnexpected ayd lent vs, in that our dangerous voyage: and so as I sayd before, we eate them by whole handfuls together, because in Holland wée had heard much spoken of their great force, and as then found it to be much more then we expected.

The 1. of August the wind blew hard North-west, and the Ice that for a while had driuen towards the entry of the Weigats, stayed and draue no more, but the sea went very hollow, wherby we were forced to remoue our Scutes on the other side of the Iland, to defend them from the waues of the sea, and lying there we went on land againe to fetch more Leple leaues, whereby wée had bin so wel holpen, & stil more and more recouered our healths, and in so short time, that we could not choose but wonder thereat, so that as then some of vs could eate bisket againe, which not long before they could not do.

The 2. of August it was dark misty weather, the wind stil blowing stiffe northwest, at which time our victuals began to decrease, for as then we had nothing but a little bread and water, and some of vs a little chéese, which made vs long sore to be gone frō thence, specially in regard of our hunger, whereby our weake members began to be much weaker, and yet we were forced to labour sore, which were two great contraries: for it behoued vs rather to haue our bellies full, that so we might be the stronger, to indure our labour, but patience was our point of trust.

The 3. of August, about the North sun, the weather being somwhat better, we agréed amongst our selues to leaue Noua Zembla

and

and to crosse ouer to Russia, and so committing our selues to God, we set saile with a North-west wind, & sailed South South-west till the Sun was east, and then we entred into Ice againe, which put vs in great feare, for we hadcrost ouer and left the Ice vpon Noua Zembla, & were in good hope y we should not meet with any Ice againe, in so short space, at which time being in the Ice, with calme weather, whereby our Sailes could doe vs no great good, we stroke our sailes and began to row againe, and at last we rowed cleane through the Ice, not without great & sore labour, and about the South-west Sunne got cleere thereof, and entred into the large sea, where we saw no Ice, and then what with sailing and rowing we had made 20. miles, & so sailing forwards we thought to aproch neere vnto the Russian coast; but about the North-west Sunne, we entred into Ice againe, and then it was very cold, wherewith our hearts became very heauy, fearing that it would alwaies contineiw in that sort, and that we should neuer be freed thereof, and for that our boate could not make so good way, nor was not able to saile aboue the point of Ice, we were compelled to enter into the Ice, for that being in it, we perceiued open sea beyond it, but the hardest matter was to get into it, for it was very close, but at last we found a meanes to enter, and got in, and being entred it was somewhat better, and in the end with great paine and labour we got into the open water: our Maister that was in the scute, which sailed better then our boate got aboue the point of the Ice, and was in some feare that we were inclosed with y Ice, but God sent vs the meanes to get out from it, as soone as he could saile about the point thereof, and so we met together againe.

The 4 of August, about the South-east Sunne, being gotten out of the Ice, we sailed forward with a North-west wind, and held our course Southerly, and when the Sunne was South, at noone time we saw the coast of Russia, lying before vs, whereat we were exceeding glad, and going neerer vnto it, we stroke our sailes and rowed on land, and found it to be very low land, like a bare strand that might be flowed ouer with the water; there we lay till the Sun was South-west, but perceiuing that there we could not much further our selues, hauing as then sailed from the point of Nouo Zembla, (from whence we put off) thither, ful 30 miles, we sailed forward along by the coast of Russia. with an indifferet gale of
wind

wind, and when the Sunne was North, we saw another Russian Iolls or ship, which we sailed vnto to speake with them, and being hard by them, they came al aboue hatches, and we cried vnto them Candinaes Candinaes (whereby we asked them if we were about Candinaes) but they cryed againe and sayd pitzora Pitzora (to shew vs that we were there abouts) & for y̌ we sailed along by the coast, where it was very drie, supposing that we held our course, west and by North, that so we might get beyond the point of Candinaes, we were wholy deceiued by our compas, that stood vpon a chest boūd wt yron bands, which made vs vary at least 2. points, whereby we were much more southerly thē we thougth our course had bin, & also farre more easterly, for we thought verily that we had not bin farre from Candinaes, and we were three daies sailing from it, as afer we perceiued, & for that we found our selues to be so much out of our way, we stayed there all night til day appeared.

The 5. of August, lying there, one of our men went on shore, and found the land further in, to be greene, and ful of trees, & from thence called to vs, to bid vs bring our peeces on shore, saying that there was wild deere to be killed, which made vs exceeding glad, for then our victuales were almost spent, and we had nothing but some broken bread, whereby we were wholy out of comfort, and some of vs were of opinion that we should leaue the Scutes, and goe further into the land, or else they said, we should all die with hunger, for that many daies before we were forced to fast, and hunger was a sharpe sword, which we could hardly endure any longer.

The 6. of August, the weather began to be somewhat better, at which time we determined to row forward because the wind was against vs, that we might get out of the creeke, the wind being East South-east which was our course as then, and so hauing rowed about three miles we could get no further, because it was so full in the wind, and we al together heartlesse and faint; the land streatching further North-east then we made account it had done, whereupon we beheld each other in pittifull manner, for we had great want of victuals, and knew not how farre we had to saile before we should get any releefe, for al our victuals was almost consumed.

The 7. of August, the wind being west North west, it serued

T3　　　　　　　　　　vs

vs well to get out of that créeke, and so we sailed forward East, and by North, till we got out of the créeke, to the place, and the point of land, where we first had bin, and there we made our Scutes fast againe: for the North-west wind was right against vs, whereby our mens hearts and courages were wholy abated, to sée no issue, how we should get from thence: for as then sicknesses, hunger, and no means to be found how to get from thence, consumed both our flesh and our bloud, but if we had found any reléefe, it would haue bin better with vs.

The 8. of August, there was no better weather, but still the wind was against vs, and we lay a good way one from the other, as we found best place for vs, at which time there was most dislike in our boate, in regard that some of vs were excéeding hungrie, and could not endure it any longer, but were wholy out of heart still wishing to die.

The 9. of August, it was all one weather, so that the wind blowing contrary, we were forced to lye still, and could goe no further, our gréese still increasing more & more, at last two of our men went out of the Scute, wherein the Maister was, which we perceiuing, two of our men also landed, and went altogether about a mile into the countrie, and at last saw a banke, by the which there issued a great streame of water, which we thought to be the way from whence the Russians came, betwéene Candinaes & the firme land of Russia, and as our men came backe againe, in the way as they went a long, they found a dead sea-horse, that stanke excéedingly, which they drew with thē to our Scute, thinking that they should haue a dainty morsell out of it, because they endured so great hunger, but we told thē that without doubt it would kil vs, & that it were better for vs, to endure pouerty and hunger for a time, then to venture vpon it, saying, that séeing God who in so many great extremitys had sent vs a happie issue, stil liued, and was excéeding powerfull, we hoped and nothing doubting, that he would not altogether forsake vs, but rather helpe vs, when we were most in dispaire.

The 10. of August, it was stil a North-west wind with mistie & darke weather, so that we were driuen to lie still, at which time it was no néed for vs to aske one another how we fared, for we could well gesse it by our countenances.

The

The 11. of Auguſt, in the mo2ning, it was faire calme weather, ſo that the Sunne being about no2th-eaſt, the maſter
ſent one of his men to vs, to bid vs p2epare our ſelues to ſet ſaile,
but we had made our ſelues ready thereunto befo2e he came, and
began to rowe towards him, at which time fo2 that I was very
weake and no longer able to rowe, as alſo fo2 that our boate
was harder to rowe then the Scute, I was ſet in the Scute, to
guide the helme, and one that was ſtronger, was ſent out of the
Scute into the boate to rowe in my place, that we might kéepe
company together, and ſo we rowed till ꝑ Sunne was ſouth, and
then we had a good gale of wind out of the ſouth, which made vs
take in our oares, and then we hoiſed vp our ſailes, wherewith
we made good way, but in the euening the wind began to blowe
hard, whereby we were fo2ced to take in our ſailes and to rowe
towards the land, where we laid our Scutes vpon the Strand,
and went on land to ſéeke fo2 freſh water, but found none, and
becauſe we could goe no further, we laid our ſailes ouer the boates
to couer vs from the weather, at which time it began to raine
very hard, and at midnight it thund2ed, and lightned, with
mo2e ſto2e of raine, where with our company were much diſ-
quieted, to ſée that they found no meanes of reléeſe, but ſtill entred into further trouble and danger.

The 12. of Auguſt, it was faire weather, at which time the
Sunne being eaſt, we ſaw a Ruſſia Lodgie come towards vs, with
al his ſailes vp, wherewith we were not a little comfo2ted, which
we perceauing from the ſtrand, where we laie with our Scutes,
we deſired the maſter that we might goe vnto him, to ſpeake
with him, and to get ſome victuales of them, and to that end
we made as much haſte as we could, to launche out our Scutes
and ſailed toward them, and when we got to them, the maſter
went into the Lodgie, to aſke them how farre we had to Cardinaes, which we could not well learne of them, becauſe we vnderſtood them not, they held vp their fiue fingers vnto vs, but
we knew not what they ment thereby, but after we perceaued,
that thereby they would ſhew vs, that there ſtood fiue Croſſes v-
pon it, and they b2ought their compas out and ſhewed vs that
it lay No2th weſt fró vs, which our compas alſo ſhewed vs, which
reckning alſo we had made: but when we ſaw we could haue no
                                                                better

better intelligence from them, the master went further into their ship, & pointed to a barrell of fish y he saw therein, making signes to know, whether they would sel it vnto vs, showing them a péece of 8. royles, which they vnderstanding, gaue vs 102. fishes, with some cakes, which they had made of meale, when they sod their fishe, and about the south Sunne we left them, being glad that we had gotten some victuales, for long before we had had but two ounces of bread a day, with a little water and nothing else, and with that we were forced to comfort our selues as well as we could: the fishes we shared amongst vs equally, to one as much as another, without any difference, & when we had left thē, we held our course west and by north, with a south, and a south and by east wind, and when the Sunne was west-south west it began to thunder and raine, but it continued not long, for shortly after the weather began to cleare vp againe, and passing for-ward in that sort, we saw the Sunne in our common Compas, go downe north and by west.

The 13. of August, we had the wind against vs, being west-south-west, and our course was west and by north, whereby we were forced to put to the shore againe, where two of our men went on the land, to sée how it laie, and whether the point of Candinaes reacht not out from thence into the sea, for we gess that we were not farre from it, our men comming againe, show-ed vs that they had séene a house vpon the land, but no man in it, and said further that they could not perceaue, but that it was the point of Candinaes that we had séene, wherewith we were some-what comforted, and went into our Scutes againe, and rowed along by the land, at which time hope made vs to be of good cōfort, & procured vs to doe more then we could well haue done, for our liues and maintenance consisted therein, and in that sort row-ing along by the land: we saw an other Russian Iollie lying v-pon the shore, which was broken in péeces, but we past by it, and a little after that, we saw a house at the water-side, where-unto some of our men went, wherein also they found no man, but onely an ouen, and when they came againe to the Scute, they brought some leple leaues with them which they had found as they went, and as we rowed along by the point, we had a good gale of winde out of the east, at which time we hoised vp our

sailes

sailes, & sailed foreward, and after none, about the south-west
Sunne, we perceaued that the point, which we had séene, laid
south-ward, whereby we were fully perswaded that it was the
point of Candinaes, fró whence we went to saile ouer the mouth
of the white sea, and to that end we borded each other and deuided our candles, and all other things that we should néed amongst
vs, to helpe our selues therewith, and so put of from the land,
thinking to passe ouer the white sea, to the coast of Russia, and
sailing in that sort, with a good winde, about midnight there rose
a great storme out of the north, wherewith we stroke saile, and
made it shorter, but our other boate that was harder vnder saile,
(knowing not that we had lessened our sailes,) sailed foreward,
whereby we straid one from the other, for then it was very
darke.

The 14. of August, in the morning, it being indifferent good
weather with a south-west wind, we sailed west north-west,
and then it began to cleare vp, so that we saw our boate, and did
what we could to get vnto her, but we could not, because it began to be mistie weather againe, and therefore we said vnto each
other, let vs hold on our course, we shal finde them well enough,
on the north coast, when we are past the white sea, our course
was west-north-west, the wind being south-west and by west,
and about the south-west Sunne, we could get no further, because the wind fel contrary, whereby we were forced to strike our
sailes, and to row foreward, and in that sort rowing till the
Sunne was west, there blew an indifferent gale of wind out of
the east and therewith we set saile, and yet we rowed with two
oares, till the Sunne was north-north-west, and then the wind
began to blow somewhat stronger east, and east-south-east, at
which time we tooke in our oares, and sailed forward west-north-
west.

The 15. of August, wée saw the sunne rise east north-east,
whereupon we thought that our compasse varied somewhat, and
when the sunne was east, it was calme weather againe, wherewith we were forced to take in our sailes, and to row againe, but
it was not long before wee had a gale of winde out of the south-
east, and then we hoysed vp our sailes againe, and went forward
west and by south, and sayling in that manner, with a good fore-
winde

And, when the ſunne was South we ſaw land, thinking that as then we had béene on the weſt ſide of the white ſea, beyond Candinaes, and being cloſe vnder the land, we ſaw ſire Ruſſian Lodgies, lying there, to whom we ſailed, and ſpake with them, aſking them how farre wée were from Kilduin, but although they vnderſtood vs not well, yet they made vs ſuch ſignes that we vnderſtood by them that we were ſtill farre from thence, and that we were yet on the Eaſt ſide of Candinaes & with that they ſtroke their hands together, thereby ſignifying y̆ we muſt firſt paſſe ouer the white ſea, and that our Scutes were to little to doe it, and that it would be ouer great daunger for vs to paſſe ouer it, with ſo ſmall Scutes and that Candinaes was ſtill North-weſt from vs, then wée aſked them for ſome bread, and they gaue vs a loafe, which wée eate hungerly vp as wée were rowing, but wée would not beléeue them, that we were ſtill on the eaſt ſide of Cardinaes,

12 we thought verily that wee had paſt ouer the white ſea, and when we left them, we rowed along by the land, the wind béeing North, and about the North-weſt ſunne, we had a good wind againe from the South-eaſt, and therewith we ſayled along by the ſhore, and ſaw a great Ruſſian Lodgie, lying on the Starreboord from vs, which we thought came out of the white ſea.

The 16. of Auguſt in the morning, ſayling forward Northweſt, wée perceiued that we were in a Créeke, & ſo made towards y̆ Ruſſian Lodgie, which we had ſéene on our ſtarrsboord, which at laſt with great labour and much paine, we got vnto, and comming to them about the South eaſt ſunne, with a hard wind, we aſked them how farre we were from Sembla de Cool or Kilduin, but they ſhooke their heads, and ſhewed vs that we were on the eaſt ſide of Zembla de Candinaes, but we would not beléeue them, and then we aſked them ſome victuals, wherewith they gaue vs certaine plaice, for the which the maiſter gaue them a péece of money, and ſailed from them againe, to get out of that hole, where wée were, as it reacht into the ſea; but they perceiuing that we tooke a wrong courſe, and that the flood was almoſt paſt, ſent two men vnto vs, in a ſmall boate, with a great loafe of bread which they gaue vs, and made ſignes vnto vs to come aboord of their ſhip againe, for that they intended to haue further ſpéech with vs, and to help vs, which we ſeeming not to refuſe, and deſiring not to be

vn

vnthankfull, gaue them a péece of money, and a péece of linnen
cloth, but they ſtayed ſtill by vs, and they that were in the grea-
Lodgie, held vp bacon and butter vnto vs, to moue vs to come a
boord of them againe, and ſo we did : and being with them, they
ſhewed vs that we were ſtil on the eaſt ſide of the point of Candinaes, then we fetcht our card and let them ſée it, by the which they
ſhewed vs, that we were ſtill on the eaſt ſide of the white ſea, and
of Cardinaes, which we vnderſtanding, were in ſome doubt with
our ſelues, becauſe we had ſo great a voiage to make ouer the
white ſea, and were in more feare for our companions that were
in the boate, as alſo ÿ hauing ſailed 22.miles along by the Ruſſian
coaſt, we had gotten no further, but were then to ſaile ouer the
mouth of the white ſea, with ſo ſmall prouiſion, for which cauſe
the maſter bought of ÿ Ruſſians thrée ſacks w̄ meale, two ſitches
and a halfe of bacon, a pot of Ruſſia butter, and a runlet of honny
for prouiſion for vs and our boate, when we ſhould méet with it a-
gaine, & for ÿ in the meane time, the flood was paſt, we ſailed with
the ebbe, out of the aforeſaid Créeke, where the Ruſſians boate
came to vs, and entred into the ſea with a good South-eaſt wind,
holding our courſe North north-weſt, and there we ſaw a point
that reacht out into the ſea, which we thought to be Candinaes,
but we ſailed ſtill forward, and the land reached North-weſt: in
the euening the ſunne being North-weſt: when we ſaw that we
did not much good with rowing, and that the ſtreame was almoſt
paſt, we lay ſtill, and ſod a pot full of water and meale, which taſted excéeding well, becauſe we had put ſome bacon fat and honny
into it, ſo that we thought it to be a feaſtiuall day with vs, but
ſtill our minds ran vpon our boate, becauſe we knew not where it
was.

The 17. of Auguſt lying at anchor, in the morning at breake of
day, we ſaw a Ruſſian Lodgie that came ſayling out of the white
ſea, to whom we rowed, that we might haue ſome inſtruction frō
him, and when wée borded him, without aſking or ſpeaking vnto him, he gaue vs a loafe of bread, and by ſignes ſhewed vs as
well as he could, that he had ſéene our companions, and that there
was ſeuen men in the boate, but we not knowing well what they
ſayd, neither yet beléeuing them, they made other ſignes vnto vs,
and held vp their ſeuen fingers, and pointed to our Scute, there

by

by ſhewing that there was ſo many men in the boate, and that they had ſold them bread, fleſh, fiſh, and other victualls: and while we ſtaid in their Lodgie, we ſaw a ſmall compaſſe therein, which we knew that they had bought of our chiefe Boatſon, which they likewiſe acknowledged, then we vnderſtanding ꝍem well, aſkt them how long it was ſince they ſaw our boats, and where-abouts it was, they made ſignes vnto vs, that it was the day be-fore: and to conclude, they ſhewed vs great friendſhip, for the which we thanked them, and ſo being glad of the good newes wée had heard, we tooke our leaues of them, much reioycing that wée heard of our companions welfare, and ſpecially becauſe they had gotten victuals from the Ruſſians, which was the thing that wée moſt doubted of, in regard that wée knew what ſmall prouiſion they had with them, which done, we rowed as hard as we could, to try if we might ouertake them, as being ſtill in doubt, that they had not prouiſion inough, wiſhing that they had had part of ours: and hauing rowed al that day with great labour along by the land, about midnight we found a fall of freſh water, and then we went on land to fetch ſome, and there alſo we got ſome Leple leaues, and as we thought to row forward, we were forced to ſaile, be-cauſe the flood was paſt, and ſtill wee lookt earneſtly out for the point of Cardinaes, and the fiue Croſſes, whereof we had béene inſtructed by the Ruſſians, but we could not ſée it.

The 18. of Auguſt in the morning, the ſunne being Eaſt, wée puld vp our ſtone, (which we vſed in ſtéed of an anchor) and row-ed along by the land, till the ſunne was ſouth, and then wée ſaw a point of land, reaching into the ſea, and on it certaine ſignes of croſſes, which as we went néerer vnto, wee ſaw perfectly, and when the ſunne was weſt, wee perceiued that the land reached Weſt and South-weſt, ſo that thereby we knew it certainly to be the point of Candinaes, lying at the mouth of the white ſea, which we were to croſſe, and had long deſired to ſée it: This point is eaſily to be knowne, hauing fiue croſſes ſtanding vpon it, which are perfectly to be decerned, one the Eaſt ſide, in the South eaſt, and one the other ſide in the South-weſt, and when we thought to ſaile from thence, to the Weſt ſide of the white ſea towards the coaſt of Norway, we found that one of our runlets of freſh water was almoſt leakt out, and for that we had about 40. Duch miles
to

to saile ouer the sea, befo2e we should get any fresh water, we sought meanes first to row on land, to get some, but because the waues wet so high we durst not do it, & so hauing a good no2th-east wind,(which was not fo2 vs to slack) we set fo2ward in the name of G D D, and when the Sunne was No2th-west, we past the point, and all that night and the next day sailed with a good wind, and all that time rowed but while th2ee glasses were run out, and the next night after ensuing, hauing still a good wind, in the mo2ning about the East No2th-east Sunne, we saw land, one the West side of the whit sea, which we found by the rushing of the sea vpon the land,befo2e we saw it,and perceiuing it to be ful of clifts,and not low sandy ground with same hils,as it is on the east side of the white sea, we assured our selues that we were on ŷ west side of the white sea, vpon the coast of Lapeland, fo2 the which we thanked G D D, that he had helped vs to saile ouer the white sea in thirty houres,it being fo2ty Dutch miles at the least,our course being West with a No2th-east wind

The 20. of August, being not farre from the land, the No2th-east wind left vs, and then it began to blow stiffe No2th-west, at which time seeing we could not make much way by sailing fo2-ward,we determined to put in betweene certaine clifts,and when we got close to the land, we espied certaine crosses, with warders vpon them, whereby we vnderstood, that it was a good way, and so put into it, and being entred a litle way within it, we saw a great Russian lodgie lying at an ancho2, whereunto we rowed as fast as we could, and there also we saw certaine houses wherein men dwelt, and when we got to the Lodgie, we made our selues fast vnto it, and cast our tent ouer the Scute, fo2 as then it began to raine, then we went on land into the houses that stood vpon the sho2e, where they shewed vs great friendship, leading vs into their stoawes, and there d2ied our wet clothes, and then seething some fish, bade vs sit downe and eate somwhat with them. In those lit-tle houses we found thirteene Russians who euery mo2ning went out to fish in the sea, whereof two of them had charge ouer the rest, they liued very poo2ely and o2dinarily eate nothing but fish & b2ead:at euening when we p2epared our selues to go to our scute againe, they p2ayed the maister and me to stay with them in their houses, which the maister thanked them fo2,would not do, but I

W 3   staied

ſtayed with them al that night : beſides thoſe thirtǽne men, there was two Laplanders moꝛe, and thꝛǽ women with a child, that liued very pooꝛely of the ouerp us which the Ruſſians gaue them, as a pǽce of fiſh, and ſome fiſhes heades, which the Ruſſians thꝛew away, and they with great thankfulneſſe toke them vp, ſo that in reſpect of their pouertie, we thought our ſelues to bee well furniſhed : ꝑ yet we had litttle inough, but as it ſǽmed, their oꝛdinary liuing was in that manner, and we were foꝛced to ſtay there, foꝛ that the wind being Noꝛthweſt, it was againſt vs.

The 21. of Auguſt it rained moſt part of the day, but not ſo much after dinner as befoꝛe, then our maſter bꝛought god ſtoꝛe of freſh fiſh, which we ſod, and eate our bellies full, which in long time we had not done, and therewith ſod ſome meale and water, in ſtǽd of bꝛead, whereby we were well comfoꝛted. After nœne, when the raine began to leſſen, we went further into the land, ant ſought foꝛ ſome Leple leaues, and then we ſaw two men vpon ꝥ hilles, whereupon we ſaid one to the other, hereabouts there muſ moꝛe people dwel, foꝛ there came two men towards vs, but w regarding them not, went backe againe to our Scute, and tc wards the houſes: the two men that were vpon the hilles (bein ſome of our men that were in the bœt꞉) perceauing the Ruſſia lodgie, came downe the hill towards her, to buy ſome victuale of them, who being come thither vnawares, and hauing no mo ny about them, they agrǽd betwǽne them to put off one of thei paire orbꝛeches, (foꝛ that as then we ware two oꝛ thꝛǽ paire on ouer the other)to ſel them foꝛ ſome victuales, but when they cam downe the hill, and were ſomewhat nǽrer vnto vs, they eſpiei our Scute lying by the lodgie, and we as then beheld them better and knew them, wherewith we reioyced, and ſhewed each o ther of our pꝛocǽdings, and how we had ſailed to and fro in greaꞇ neceſſitie and hunger, and yet they had bǽne in greater neceſſitiꞇ and danger then we, and gaue God thankes, that he had pꝛeſer ued vs aliue, and bꝛought vs together againe, and then we eatꞇ ſome thing together, and dꝛanke of the cleare water, ſuch as run neth along by Collen thꝛough the Rem, and then we agrǽd that they ſhould come vnto vs, that we might ſaile together.

The 22. of Auguſt, the reſt of our men with the boate came vn꞉ to vs, about the Eaſt South eaſt Sunne, whereat we much reioy꞉
ced

t⁓, and then we prayed the Ruſſians cooke, to bake a ſacke of neale for vs, and to make it bread, paying him for it, which he did, and in the meane time, when the fiſhermen came with their fiſhe out of the ſea, our maiſter bought foure Cods of them, which we ſod and eate, and while we were at meat, the chiefe of the Ruſſians came vnto vs, and perceiuing that we had not much bread, he fetcht a loafe and gaue it vs, and although we deſired them to ſit downe and eate ſome meat with vs, yet we could by no means get the to graunt thereunto, becauſe it was their faſting day, & for ẏ we had poured butter and fat into our fiſh: nor we could not get them once to drinke with vs, becauſe our cup was ſomewhat greaſie, they were ſo ſuperſtitious touching their faſting, and religion, neither would they lend vs any of their cups to drinke in, leaſt they ſhould likewiſe be greaſed, at that time the wind was North-weſt.

The 23. of Auguſt, the Cooke began to knead our meale, and made vs bread thereof, which being don, and the wind and weather beginning to be ſomewhat better, we made our ſelues ready to depart from thence, at which time, when the Ruſſians came from fiſhing, our maiſter gaue their chiefe commander a good pẻece of mony, in regard of the frendſhip that he had ſhewed vs, and gaue ſome what alſo to the cooke, for the which they yẻelded vs great thankes, at which time the chiefe of the Ruſſians, deſired our maiſter to giue him ſome gunpowder which he did, and when we were ready to ſaile from thence, we put a ſacke of meale into the boate, leaſt we ſhould chance to ſtray one from the other againe, that they might help them ſelues therewith, and ſo about euening when the Sunne was Weſt, we ſet ſaile and departed from thence, when it began to be high water, & with a North-eaſt wind, held our courſe North-weſt along by the land.

The 24. of Auguſt, the wind blew Eaſt, and then the Sunne being Eaſt, we got to the ſeuen Iſlands, where we found many fiſhermen, of whom we enquired after Cool and Kilduin, and they made ſignes that they lay Weſt from vs, (which we likewiſe geſt to be ſo, (and withall they ſhewed vs great frendſhip, and caſt a Cod into our Scute, but for that we had a good gale of wind, we could not ſtay to pay them for it, but gaue them great thanks, much wondering at there great courteſy, and ſo with a good gale of wind

wind, we arriued befoze the ſeuen Iſlands, when the Sun was
South-weſt,and paſt betwæn them and the land,and there found
certaine fiſhermen,that rowed to vs,& aſked vs where our Crable
(meaning our ſhip)was, whereunto wee made anſwere with as
much Ruſſian Language as we had learned,& ſaid,Crable pro Pal
(y is our ſhip is loſt) which they vnderſtanding ſaid vnto vs, Cool
Brabouſe Crable whereby we vnderſtod that at Cool there was
certaine Þeatherland ſhips, but we made no great account therof
becauſe our intent was to ſaile to VVare-houſe, fearing leaſt
the Ruſſians oz great Þzince of the country, would ſtay vs
there.

The 25.of Auguſt, ſailing along by the land with a South-eaſt
wind, about the South Sun, we had a ſight of Kilduin, at which
time we held our courſe Weſt Þozth-weſt, and ſailing in that
manner betwéene Kilduin and the firme land, about the South
South-weſt Sunne, we got to the Weſt end of Kilduin, and being there lookt if we could ſée any houſes, oz people therein, and at
laſt we ſaw certaine Ruſſian lodgies that lay vpon the ſtrand,and
there finding a conuenient place foz vs to Anchoz with our
Scutes, while we went to know if any people were to be found,
our maiſter put in with the land, and there found fiue oz ſix ſmall
houſes, wherein the Laplanders dwelt, of whom we aſked if that
were Kilduin,whereunto they made anſwere,& ſhewed vs that it
was Kilduin, & ſaid y at Coola there lay thzée Brabants Crables
oz ſhips,whereof two were that day to ſet ſaile, which we hearing
determined to ſaile to Ware-houſe,and about the Weſt, South-
weſt ſunne, put off from thence with a South-eaſt wind : but as
we were vnder ſaile, the wind blew ſo ſtiffe, that wee durſt not
kéepe the ſea in the night time, foz that the waues of the ſea went
ſo hollow, that we were ſtill in doubt that they would ſmite the
Scutes to the ground, and ſo tooke our courſe behind two clifts,
towards the land, and when we came there, wee found a ſmall
houſe vpon the ſhoze, wherein there was thzée men and a great
dogge, which receiued vs very friendly,aſking vs of our affaires,
and how we got thither, whereunto we made anſwere,and ſhewed them that we had loſt our ſhip, and that we were come thither
to ſée if we could get a ſhip that would bzing vs into Holland :
wherunto they made vs anſwere as the other Ruſſians had done,
that

that there was thꝛ�ee ſhips at Coola, whereof two were to ſet ſaile from thence that day, then we aſked them if they would goe with one of our men by land to Coola, to looke foꝛ a ſhip, wherewith we might get into Holland, and ſaid we would reward them well foꝛ their paines, but they excuſed themſelues and ſaid, that they could not go from thence, but they ſayd that they would bꝛing vs ouer the hill, where we ſhould finde certaine Laplanders whom they thought would go with vs, as they did: foꝛ the maiſter and one of our men, going with them ouer the hill, found certaine Laplanders there, whereof they got one to go with our man, pꝛomiſing him two royals of eight foꝛ his pains, and ſo the Laplander going with him, tooke a p�eece on his necke, and our man a boate-hooke, and about euening they ſet foꝛward, the wind as then being Eaſt, and Eaſt Noꝛth-eaſt,

The 26. of Auguſt it was faire weather the wind South eaſt, at which time we dꝛew vp both our Scutes vpon the land, and tooke all the goods out of them, to make them the lighter, which done, we went to the Ruſſians and warmed vs, and there dꝛeſſed ſuch meates as we had, and then againe w�ee began to make two meales a day, when we perceiued that we ſhould euery day find moꝛe people, and we dꝛanke of their dꝛinke which they call Quas, which was made of bꝛoken p�eeces of bꝛead, and it taſted well: foꝛ in long time we had dꝛunke nothing elſe but water: ſome of our men went further into the land & there found blew berries, and bꝛamble berries, which they plucked and eate, and they did vs much good, foꝛ we found that they healed vs of our looſeneſſe, the wind ſtill blew South-eaſt.

The 27. of Auguſt, it was foule weather with a great ſtoꝛm, Noꝛth, and Noꝛth Noꝛth-weſt, ſo that in regard that the Strand was low, and as alſo foꝛ that the ſpꝛing tide was ready to come on we dꝛew our Scutes a great way vp vpon the land, which hauing done, wee went to the Ruſſians to warme vs by their fire and to dꝛeſſe our meate: meane time the maiſter ſent one of our men to the ſea ſide to our Scutes, to make a fire foꝛ vs vpon the Strand, that when we came we might finde it ready, and that in the meane time the ſmoake might be gone, and while one of our men was there, and the other was going thither, the water dꝛaue ſo high, that both our Scutes were ſmitten into the water, and in

‡ great

great danger to be cast away, for in the Scute there was but two men, and three in the boate, who with much labour and paine, could hardly keep the Scutes from being broken vpon the strand, which we seeing, were in great doubt, and yet could not help them, yet God be thanked, he had then brought vs so farre, that neuerthelesse we could haue gotten home, although wee should haue lost our Scutes, as after it was seene. That day, and all night it rained sore, whereby we indured great trouble and miserie, being throughly wet, and could neither couer nor defend our selues frõ it, and yet they in the Scutes indured much more, being forced to bee in that weather, and still in daunger to bee cast vpon the shore.

The 28. of August it was indifferent good wether, and then we drew the Scutes vpon the land againe, that we might take the rest of the goods out of them, because the wind still blew hard north, and north-north-west, and hauing drawne the Scutes vp, we spread our sailes vpon them, to shelter vs vnder them, for it was still mistie, and rainie weather, much desiring to heare some newes of our man, that was gone to Cola with the Lapelander, to know if there were any shipping at Coola to bring vs into Holland, and while we laie there we went into the land and fetch some blew berries and bramble buries to eate, which did vs much good.

The 29. of August it was indifferent faire weather, and we were still in good hope to heare some good newes from Cola, and alwaies looked vp towards the hill to see if our man and the Lapelander came, but seeing they came not, we went to the Russians againe, and there drest our meate, and then went to goe to our Scutes to lodge in them all night, in the meane time we spied the Lapelander cõming alone without our man whereat we wondred, and were somewhat in doubt, but when he came vnto vs, he shewed vs a letter that was written vnto our maister, which he opened before vs, the contents thereof being, that he that had written the letter wondred much at our arriuall in that place, and that long sence he verily thought that we had béene all cast away, being exceeding glad of our happy fortune, and how that he would presently come vnto vs, with victuales and all other necessaries to succour vs withall, we being in no small admiration

who

who it might be, that shewed vs so great fauour and friendship, could not imagine what he was, for it appeared by the letter, that he knew vs well: and although the letter wes subscribed, by ms Iohn Corneliſon Rip, yet we could not be perſwaded, that it was the ſame Iohn Corneliſon, who the yéere before had béene ſet out in the other ſhip with vs, and left vs about the Beare Iſland: for thoſe good newes we paid the Lapelander his hier, and beſide that gaue him hoaſe, bꝛeeches and other furniture, ſo that he was apparelled like a Hollander: for as then we thought our ſelues to be wholy out of danger, and ſo being of good comfoꝛt, we laid vs downe to reſt: Here I cannot chuſe but ſhew you how faſt the Lapelander went: foꝛ when he went he went to Cola, as our companion told vs, they were two dayes and two nights on the way, and yet went a pace, and when he came backe againe, he was but a day & a night cōming to vs, which was wonderful, it being but halfe ẏ time, ſo that we ſaid, & verily thought, that he was halfe a coniurer and he bꝛought vs a partridge which he had killed by the way as he went.

The 30. of Auguſt it was indifferent faire weather, we ſtill wondering who that Iohn Corneliſon might be that had wꝛitten vnto vs, and while we ſate mnſing thereon, ſome of vs were of opinion that it might be the ſame Iohn Corneliſon that had ſayled out of Hollād in company with vs, which we could not be perſwaded to beléeue, becauſe we were in as little hope of his life as hée of ours, ſuppoſing that he had ſped woꝛſe then we, and long befoꝛe that had béene caſt away, at laſt the maſter ſaid, I will looke amongſt my letters, foꝛ there I haue his name wꝛitten, and that will put vs out of doubt, & ſo looking amongſt them, we found that it was the ſame Iohn Corneliſon, wherewith we were as glad of his ſafety & welfare, as he was of ours, and while we were ſpeaking thereof, and that ſome of vs would not beléeue that it was the ſame Iohn Corneliſon, we ſaw a Ruſſian Ioll come rowing, with Iohn Corneliſon and our companion, that wee had ſent to Cola, who being landed, we receiued & welcomed each other, w great ioy & exceding gladneſſe, as if either of vs on both ſides had ſéene each other riſe from death to life again: for we eſtéemed him, & he vs to be dead long ſince: he bꝛought vs a barrell of Koſwicke béere, wine, aquauite, bꝛead, fleſh, bacon, Salmon, ſuger, and other things which comforted and releeued vs much, and wee reioyced together for our so vnexpected meeting : at that time giuing God great thankes for his mercy shewed vnto vs.

The 31. of August it was indifferent faire weather, the wind Easterly, but in the euening it began to blow hard from the land, and then we made preparation to saile from thence to Cola, first taking our leaues of the Russians, and heartily thanking them for their curtesie shewed vnto vs and gaue them a peece of money for their good wils, and at night about the North-sunne we sailed from thence with a high water.

The 1. of September in the morning, with the East sunne, we got to y west side of the riuer of Cola & entered into it, where we rowed till the flood was past, and then we cast the stones that serued vs for anchors, vpon the ground, at a point of land till the flood came in againe : and when the sunne was south, wee set saile againe with the flood, & so sailed and rowed till midnight, and then we cast anchor againe till morning

The 2. of September in the morning, we rowed vp the riuer, and as we past along we saw some trees on the riuer side, w comforted vs, and made vs as glad as if we had then come into a new world, for in all the time y we had beene out, we had not seene any trees, & when we were by the the salt kettles, which is about three miles from Cola, we stayed there a while, & made merry, & then went forward againe, and with the West, North-west san got to Iohn Cornelisons ship, wherein we entred and drunke : there wee began to make merry, againe, with the sailers that were therein, and that had beene in the voiage with Iohn Corne- lison the yeare before, and bad each other welcome : then we ro- wed forward, & late in the euening got to Cola, where some of vs went on land, and some stayed in the Scutes to looke to the goods : to whom we sent milke and other things to comfort & re- fresh them, and we were all exceeding glad that God of his mercy had deliuered vs out of so many dangers and troubles, and had brought vs thither in safety : for as then wee esteemed our selues to be safe : although y place in times past, lying so far from vs was as much vnknowne vnto vs as if it had beene out of the world, & at that time being there, we thought y we were almost at home.

The 3. of September we vnladed all our goods & there refreshed

our

out selues, after our toylesome and weary iourney, and the great hunger that we had indured, thereby to recouer our healthes and strengthes againe.

The 11. of September, by leaue and consent of the Bayart, gouernour for the great prince of Muscouia, we brought our Scute and our boate into the merchants house, and there let them stand for a remembrance of our long farre (& neuer before sailed way) and that we had sailed in those open Scutes almost 400. Dutch miles, through and along by the sea coasts to the towne of Coola, whereat the inhabitants thereof could not sufficiently wonder.

The 15. of Sep. we went in a Lodgie, with all our goods & our men to Iohn Cornelisons ship, which lay about halfe a mile from the towne, and that day sailed in the ship downe the riuer til we were beyond the narrowest part thereof which was about half the riuer, and there stated for Iohn Cornelison, and our Maister, that said they would come to vs the next day

The 17. of September Iohn Cornelison, and our Maister bebeing come abord, the next day about the East Sunne, we set saile out of the riuer Coola, & with G O D S grace put to sea, to saile hom-wards, and being out of the riuer we sailed along by the land North-west, and by North, the wind being South.

The 19. of September, about the South Sunne, we got to Ware-house, and there ankored, and went on land, because Iohn Cornelison, was there to take in more goods, and staid there til the sixt of October, in the which time we had a hard wind out of the North and North west, & while we stayed there, we refreshed our selues somewhat better, to recouer our sicknesse and weaknesse againe, that we might grow stronger, which asked sometime, for we were much spent and exceeding weake.

The 6. of October, about eueninig, the Sunne being Southwest, we set saile, and with G O D S grace from VVare house, for Holland, but for that it is a common and well knowne way, I will speake nothing thereof, only that vpon the 29. October, we ariued in the Mase, with an East north-east wind, & the next morning got to Maseland sluce, and there going on land, from thence rowed to Delfe, and then to the Hage, and from thence to Harlem, & vpon the first of Nouember about noone, got to Amsterdam, in the same clothes that we ware in Noua Zembla , with our caps

furd

furd with white Foxes skins, and went to the house of Peter Haſselaer, that was one of the marchants, that ſet out the two ships, which were conducted by Iohn Corneliſon, and our Maiſter, and being there, where many men woundzed to ſee vs, as hauing eſteemed vs long befoze that to haue bin dead and rotten, the newes thereof being ſpzead abzoad in the towne, it was alſo caried to the Pzinces courte, in the Hage, at which time the Lozd Chanceloz of Denmarke, Ambaſadoz foz the ſaid King, was then at dinner with Pzince Maurice: foz the which cauſe we were pzeſently fetcht thither by the Scout, and two of the Burgers of the towne, and there in the pzeſence of thoſe Ambaſadozs, and the Burger maiſters, we made rehearſall of our Iourney both forwards and backewards, and after that euery man that dwelt thereaoouts went home, but ſuch as dwelt not nære to that place, were placed in good lodgings foz certaine daies, vntill we had receiued our pay, and then euery one of vs departed, and went to the place of his aboad.

The names of thoſe that came home againe from this dangerous viage, were.

Iacob Hemſkeck Maiſter and Factor.
Peter Peterſon Vos.
Geret de Veer.
Maiſter Hans Vos Surgion.
Iacob Iohnſon, Sterenburg.
Lenard Hendrickſon.
Laurence VVilliamſon.
Iohn Hillbrantſon.
Iacob Iohnſon hooghwont.
Peter Corneliſon.
Iohn Vous Buyſen.
and Iacob Euartſon.

FINIS.